Better
Living

Better Living

Tips for Saving Time and Money

by Sherri Brennen

WVEC-TV, Inc.
613 Woodis Avenue
Norfolk, Virginia   23510

ISBN 1-57178-006-8

Library of Congress Catalog Card Number: 94-61866

Design by Annette Overlease and Frances Dodson

Published by WVEC-TV, Inc.

Distributed by Council Oak Books

1350 East 15th Street

Tulsa, Oklahoma   74120

1 800 247-8850

In Oklahoma, 918 587-6454

Fax 918 583-4995

Better Living began as a television news story examining the clever strategies Americans are using to cope with the new economic conditions of the '90s. The ideas for saving time and money generated an astounding number of requests for more information. In response, *Better Living* took on a new life as a weekly television feature, complete with a *Better Living* hot line. Continued viewer interest gave birth to the idea of a book—*Better Living*.

Better Living is a collection of the most popular *Better Living* television scripts, adapted for print. We've featured the topics that have generated the most interest, and embellished them with lots of extra tips.

Sherri Brennen is an Emmy award-winning broadcaster who specializes in home, family, and community issues.

Her work has been recognized for excellence by numerous groups, including the National Association of Broadcasters, the National Academy of Television Arts and Sciences, and the National Education Association. She served as chair of the ABC Network Community Relations Advisory Board and was twice named an Outstanding American Woman.

Better Living is a regular television feature based on her many interviews with experts and tested in her real life experience as a wife and working mother.

Contents

Contents

Contents

Contents

Contents

Shopping

*S*hopping can take up a lot more than cash. It's estimated that women today spend one full working day each week shopping in stores and traveling to them. That's somewhere around 400 hours a year. No question that shopping can be fun, but, like anything else, it's a skill. This section is devoted to tips and tricks to help you get the most for your money in the least amount of time.

Take a calculator. This will help you keep track of bidding and of how much you're spending.

AUCTIONS

ou've probably seen them in the movies: fast-talking auctioneers selling high-priced art and antiques. But auctions aren't limited to luxury items. You can find great bargains on just about anything at local auctions, but how much you save is largely a matter of luck and skill. Here's what you need to know.

● Do some research. Attend an auction to check out the merchandise and to get an idea of how things work. Ask about other auctions in your area.

● Start with small, local auctions where the bidding moves along slower and the items aren't as pricey.

● Educate yourself about antiques. Go to the library to learn about items that interest you. Just because something looks old doesn't necessarily mean it is an antique.

● Set a limit on what you're willing to spend and stick to it. It's easy to get caught up in the excitement of bidding, and because prices change quickly, you can easily loose track of the dollar amount.

● Check out methods of payment. Some auction houses will take cash only; others will take personal or certified checks. Be sure you understand the terms of payment before the auction starts.

● Be aware of extra expenses. There is always sales tax, and many auction houses charge a buyer's premium, which is a percentage added on to the final price.

● Be sure you know exactly what you're buying. For example, a dining room set may be sold by the piece. A single chair for $25 sounds great, but a set of six can really add up.

● Be prepared to take your bargain home. Don't wait until after you've made a purchase to try to find a way to have it delivered.

Go to the previews. What you see is what you get, so be sure to carefully inspect all items, inside and out.

● Most of all, have fun. You don't have to buy anything to enjoy the excitement of an auction, but if you do, these few tips will help make sure it's a great bargain.

Wear clothes and shoes that will allow you to try things on easily.

SECRETS OF SUCCESSFUL SALE-ING

No question about it—one of the best ways to stretch a dollar is to buy things on sale. But a good sale can also be a temptation to buy things you don't really need. Here are a few tips to help you get the most out of your bargain hunting.

● Get there early. The best bargains go to the earliest shoppers.

● Plan ahead. Make a list and shop first for things you really need. Save browsing for later.

● Understand sale jargon.

On Sale generally means the item is discounted only temporarily.

Clearance Sale generally means the price has been substantially reduced.

Special Purchase suggests not a sale at all, but an item the store acquired at a good price that they pass on to you. Beware, though, these items can sometimes be inferior to the store's regular inventory.

● Don't buy anything that doesn't fit well. It's almost never a bargain.

● Check the store's return policy. It's not unusual for sale items to be non-returnable.

● Get a rain check. Frequently a store will offer a rain check for an advertised special that's been sold out. Be sure to ask.

● And how do you know something is really a bargain? Here's a quick test.

> *Do you need it?*
>
> *Is the item well made and in perfect condition?*
>
> *Is it the right size? (This applies to more than clothing.)*
>
> *Is it at least 40% off?*
>
> *Can you pay cash, or will you have to charge it?*

If you can answer "yes" to these five questions, then you probably have a great bargain. More than one "no" indicates a shopping mistake.

SHOPPING CALENDAR

*M*onth after month, savvy shoppers stretch their budgets by shopping the sales. Even in today's crazy economy, many retailers still adhere to traditional sale dates. A shopping calendar can let you know in advance when to look for specific items.

Here's when the experts say you're most likely to find things on sale.

JANUARY

Appliances, China, Home Furnishings, Art Supplies, Bicycles, Table Linens, Costume Jewelry, Electronic Equipment, Lingerie, Bath & Bedding Supplies (White Sales)

FEBRUARY

Bedding, Curtains, Stereos, Car Seat Covers, Sportswear, Toys, Glassware, Lamps, Rugs & Carpets

MARCH

Storm Windows, Ski Equipment, Hosiery, Luggage, Children's Shoes, Children's Clothing, Winter Coats

APRIL

Dresses, Women's Hats, Infants' Wear, Men's & Boys' Suits

MAY

Blankets, Bathrobes, Tires, TV Sets, Handbags

JUNE

Furniture, Lightweight Clothing, Piece Goods, Building Materials

JULY

Air Conditioners, Fuel Oil, Children's Clothing, Home Appliances

AUGUST

New Cars, Camping Equipment, Men's Coats, Home Furnishings, Bathing Suits

SEPTEMBER

Car Batteries, Dishes, Mufflers, Paint, Housewares

OCTOBER

Fishing Equipment, Silverware, Glassware, School Supplies

NOVEMBER

Water Heaters, Quilts, Men's & Women's Shoes, Coats

DECEMBER

Gift Wrap & Christmas Cards, Decorations & Ornaments, Used Cars, Boys' Suits, Men's Clothing

If you receive the wrong merchandise, the company is responsible for the return shipping charges. Call immediately and ask how to proceed.

CATALOG SHOPPING

*M*ore than 100 million of us rely on the convenience of shopping by mail from catalogs. It can be a great time and money saver if you know how to do it right. Here are some things to keep in mind.

● Be sure you understand return policies, which should be clearly listed in the catalog. Remember that some firms won't allow returns on products that can be duplicated, like recorded music and software.

● Before making a major purchase by mail, ask the company to send you a copy of the warranty in advance. Read it carefully before you place the order. If a company refuses, it's probably not a good idea to do business with them.

● Always fill out the order form, even if you're ordering by phone. It makes ordering easier and will give you a record for your files.

● Be prepared when you place your call, and read from the form. Ask when you can expect to receive your merchandise and make a note on your calendar.

● To help keep track of things, write the company's phone number on your calendar on the date you place an order. Then you'll have a reminder of when you placed an order and how to reach the company if you have a question.

● If you're paying by check, use the lower left corner to jot down your order number and the items. This way, if you receive the cancelled check and no merchandise, you'll have a record of it.

● When shopping for clothes, it's a good idea to order everything that interests you at once. That way, you can try things on, see what fits, and return the rest in one step. Many people order bit by bit and often neglect to return things because it becomes such a hassle.

Of course, you should never send cash through the mail.

● If you receive damaged merchandise, save the packing material and call the company. It should send you a replacement immediately and alert the shipping company to pick up the damaged order.

● The company should handle refunds in the same way you paid. Charges should be credited within one billing cycle and checks or money orders should be issued within seven business days.

● If you have a problem that can't be solved over the phone, you can write to:

Mail Order Action Line
Direct Marketing Association
1101 17th St., NW, #705
Washington, D.C. 20036-4704

Make sure garments are clean and in good repair. The newer-looking the garment, the quicker it will sell.

CONSIGNMENT SHOPS

*G*etting the most for your money doesn't always stop with buying. More and more, experienced penny pinchers are recycling their old items and making money through consignment shops. It works like this:

Consignment shops will accept good quality, used items and place them for sale in their showrooms. When the item sells, you split the money, usually 50/50. Here are a few tips.

● Shops accept clothing seasonally. There's little demand for a winter coat in June.

● Take your clothes early in the season. The earlier you can get your clothes on the rack, the better your chance of making a sale.

● Check out different shops. Get a feel for the stores that feature the type of items you have to sell.

● Specialty clothes sell best. Party dresses, formals, suits, and good coats are the first off the racks.

● Replace worn bows, buttons, or other decorative items. A small investment can make an item appear a lot more valuable.

● Remember that consignment shops are not thrift stores. They carry only gently used, good quality merchandise.

● Not everything will sell. Most shops will donate to charity anything that doesn't sell within a specified period of time.

COUPONS

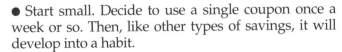

*H*ow would you like to cut your family grocery bill by 7% to 10%? Statistics show that the average shopper can do it by using coupons. Trouble is, most of us aren't interested in clipping and sorting just to save a few cents. But there are a few basic things you can do without much hassle. Here are some ideas to take advantage of coupons without going overboard.

Keep your coupons in the car. The next time you need to make a quick stop after work, you'll have your coupons handy.

● Start small. Decide to use a single coupon once a week or so. Then, like other types of savings, it will develop into a habit.

● Keep it simple. The most common reason people stop using coupons is because it gets overwhelming.

● Clip only for products you already use. Don't even bother with coupons for brands that are similar to your favorites. Save experimentation for when you become more coupon savvy.

● Try to get several coupons for the same items. Ask your neighbors for the coupon section when they're through with the paper. Now, instead of a single coupon for your favorite soup, you have enough to buy several at a good price.

● Match coupons to a sale price. This is the way the real diehards maximize their savings.

● File coupons according to basic categories, such as dairy, meat, baking supplies, and cleaning products.

● Don't just stuff coupons in a box. Keep them in a divided envelope or invest in an inexpensive coupon organizer.

Buy smaller sizes. Couponing experts say it's nearly always a better deal to use two coupons on two small sizes than a single coupon for a larger size.

● Get the most out of your efforts by planning ahead for stockpiling opportunities. Collect several coupons for an item you always need on hand—such as paper towels. Then watch carefully for a sale, especially at a store that doubles coupons. This way you can buy a dozen items or so and save a big chunk at once. Even if this is the only couponing you do, it's worth the trouble.

● Buy a big city newspaper once a week. Often, large newspapers have a bigger and better selection of coupons. These newspapers are fun to read and you can get more than your money back in additional coupon savings.

● Don't hesitate to allow coupons to expire. It's better to toss a coupon than to use it on something you don't need at the time. Besides, new coupons for the same products are frequently issued right after the expiration dates of existing ones.

● Highlight expiration dates. Use coupons with the earliest expiration dates first.

● Develop a weekly routine. Ten minutes every Sunday morning is much more likely to result in significant savings than leaving coupon clipping and filing to chance.

● Don't run from store to store to use a single coupon or two. You're better off in the long run to use your coupons at a store that seems to have the best values week after week. The less complicated couponing is, the more likely you'll stick with it, and the more money you'll save over time.

● Give your kids the money. If you can't bring yourself to deal with coupon clipping, promise your kids the money you save if they do the clipping and organizing. You'll still save in the long run.

GROCERY STORE SAVVY

*C*ornell University researchers have determined that an average shopper can cut his or her grocery bill by 15% simply by being more aware and informed. Combine basic knowledge with a few clever tricks, and who knows how much you can save? Here's a list of some saving strategies that really work. Some may be tips you already use, but you might find a few new ones to help you save even more.

Buy store brand basics. Store brand products such as rice, sugar, flour, and other basics are usually the same as more expensive national brands.

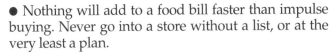

● Nothing will add to a food bill faster than impulse buying. Never go into a store without a list, or at the very least a plan.

● Choose a favorite grocery store. Dashing from store to store rarely saves money in the long run. Find a convenient store that has good prices on the things you use every week and stick with it.

● Be careful when companion foods are on display. The tuna may be discounted, but the mayonnaise could be premium priced.

● Don't assume a bright display means a sale. Aisle end displays of products are often regular price or even higher.

● Check top and bottom shelves. More expensive merchandise is often placed at eye level.

● Don't assume the large size is cheaper. Check the unit pricing information to determine the best buy.

● Check the newspaper for sales. Supermarkets often negotiate a genuinely lower price on certain products and can pass the savings on to you.

Buy butter on sale and freeze it. Salted butter will keep for about nine months.

● Buy basics in bulk. Rice, sugar and similar products have a very long shelf life. But be realistic about how much your family will use.

● Weigh all bagged produce to get the most for your money. Two bags of apples can cost the same but differ in weight by as much as half a pound.

● Don't judge size by looks. Weigh heads of lettuce, stalks of celery, bunches of carrots, and other produce to be sure you're getting the most for your money.

● Avoid convenience foods such as shredded vegetables or cheese. You pay a great deal extra for work you can easily do yourself.

● Buy plain frozen vegetables and add butter or sauce yourself.

● Fresh carrots are nearly always cheaper than frozen or canned.

● Instant mashed potatoes are usually less expensive than fresh.

● Expect about a 45% waste if you discard the skin on chicken breasts. Boneless and skinless breasts may be a better buy.

● Compare the prices of packaged luncheon meats with deli-sliced meats. One is not necessarily cheaper than the other.

● A heavier turkey will give you more meat for the money. As a general rule, a 20 pound bird has more meat per pound than one that weighs 15 pounds.

● Check all "sell by" and "use by" dates. Make sure you plan to use the food before expiration.

● Frozen orange juice is often more expensive per ounce than large, ready-to-drink cartons. Check the prices carefully.

● Not all convenience foods are the most expensive. Sometimes cake, brownie, and muffin mixes can be cheaper than homemade.

● Buy a frozen entre to keep on hand for busy days. Even pricey frozen meals are usually less expensive than take out.

● Be careful of gourmet items. The premium price is often a function of style rather than substance. Look for a less glamorous substitute.

Make your own salad dressing. Even the dry mix is cheaper than the bottled type.

Make a list. Shop first for items you need, save browsing for later.

OUTLET SHOPPING

*O*n average, shoppers are saving 25% to 50% on current-season, first-quality merchandise by shopping outlet centers. True outlets are shops owned by the same company that manufactures the goods. This essentially eliminates the middleman and allows for greater savings. The success of these stores has also made way for less reputable merchants who offer lower quality merchandise at a meager savings. Outlet shopping offers an opportunity for great bargains, but as always—"buyer beware."

● Shop with a friend. You'll probably want some help with buying decisions.

● Start in the back of the store. More expensive and, therefore, more profitable merchandise is traditionally placed up front. Bargains are tucked away in the back.

● Look for solid colors. Prints and designs are the first things to look dated. This applies to clothing, tableware, bedding, and other housewares.

● Check warranties carefully. The length and quality of a warranty is an important consideration when you purchase discounted merchandise.

● Understand the return policy. Policies can vary widely from store to store, so it's always best to check.

● Keep your receipt. A receipt will make returns and exchanges much easier, should the product turn out to be less than you expected.

● Understand labels. Experts say that about 80% of outlet merchandise is first quality, but some of the best buys are slightly flawed. Here's what the labels mean.

Irregular—Tiny imperfections, no serious flaws.

Seconds—This is flawed merchandise. It's usually pretty good but needs to be carefully inspected.

Past Season—Last year's styles are this year's best bargains.

Samples—These have been on display and can be shopworn. Colors don't always match coordinating pieces and cuts and sizes are limited.

Discontinued—These are the items that will no longer be manufactured.

Some of the best buys in pawn shops include musical instruments, tools, silver, jewelry, and electronics.

PAWN SHOPS

*A*lthough there are few "steals" left in the world, you can still find a few great deals. Pawn shops offer a wide selection of merchandise at prices well below retail. Because they still have something of an image problem, there's less competition from other bargain hunters. Many pawn shops have worked hard to become more mainstream and accessible. So it's a good idea to check them out, especially if you have a specific item in mind. Here's what you need to know to get started.

● Shop around. Check prices for a specific item so you can accurately compare costs when you visit a pawn shop.

● Expect significant savings. Most good pawn shops offer items in the neighborhood of 40% to 50% off retail and even more, although many items can vary.

● Ask if the store will take a trade. Some shops will take merchandise as trade toward the purchase price of another item. You might be able to get a new CD player for a few dollars plus the trade of your old tape machine.

● Ask if merchandise comes with a guarantee or warranty. A lot of the merchandise offered in pawn shops is new or reconditioned and may be guaranteed.

● Prices can change every day. Shop often because pawn shops operate a little like the stock market. Prices go up and down for various reasons.

● No offer is foolish. It can't hurt to make a sincere offer of any price. They can say "no," but occasionally they need to move certain merchandise at a much lower cost.

● Remember the law of supply and demand. If the shop has several of the same items that have been on the floor for a while, you're more likely to get a better price.

● Establish a relationship with a pawn shop. Many shops will be happy to look out for a particular item and call you when it becomes available.

● Know what you're willing to spend. Everyone understands budgets, and a good pawn shop can help you work with the money you have.

Try negotiating. It's not unreasonable to offer 5% to 10% less than the asking price.

Nearly all store brand aluminum foil is the same. Most foil is made by one of two national companies and is likely to be of the same quality as national brands.

STORE BRANDS

Store brands have come a long way from the unreliable generic products that first appeared in the '70s. Actually, today's store brands—products that bear the name of the retail store—are copies of national brand products. They're similar to knock-offs in the fashion industry. It's not really true that national companies simply switch labels as identical products move down the production line, but many store brands are remarkably similar to leading brands. Here's how it works.

Independent manufacturers analyze popular products and try to duplicate them. Since recipes and formulas are top secret, the process is one of trial and error.

The goal is to reproduce or surpass the quality of the national brand. Then, because there is little research, development, marketing, or advertising cost, the product can be delivered to store shelves for less. Good deal? Well, sometimes. Here's what you need to know.

● Always try the store brand at least once. If you like it, you'll enjoy the savings. If you don't, just chalk it up to research.

● Store brand commodities are nearly always the best buy. Commodities are basic things that don't require a recipe—such as sugar, rice, flour, and plain frozen vegetables.

● Store brand paper products offer good savings. These products differ in texture and appearance from national brands because they're often made from recycled material. For many people, this is a plus.

● Store brand plastic wraps are not copies of the most popular national products. Because of patent restrictions, the most popular plastic wrap is not available in a store brand. The savings may not be worth the difference in quality.

● Watch for downsizing. To compete with the lower-priced store brands, some national brands have cut back on the amount of product while keeping the same package size and price. Consumers may think they're getting a full pound when, in fact, the amount has been cut back to 14 ounces.

● Watch for packaging similarities. This is the manu-facturer's way of letting you know which product has been copied. Similar package—similar product.

● Consider packaging when you buy. One area where store brands tend to fall behind is in packag-ing. If the package is important to the use of the prod-uct, such as aluminum foil, be sure to check it out. Nothing is more frustrating than a full role of foil and a poorly designed tear strip that won't cut.

Specify that items should be in good condition. Make sure that people understand that it's not a junk swap.

SWAP PARTIES

*R*emember swap meets? All the rage in the '50s, they're back and revamped. Instead of the old-fashioned flea market format, contemporary swaps are set up like parties where friends bring items they no longer use and trade them. Usually there's a theme—such as toys, clothes or cookware. It's a great way to clean out closets and get some new, fun things in the process. Here are a few things to keep in mind.

● Decide on a theme. Good choices are toys, kids' clothes, costume jewelry, beauty supplies, women's clothes, cookbooks, kitchen utensils, tools, and books.

● Invite people who are friendly with one another and can share generously.

● Stack items in a pile and cover them with a blanket. This prevents peeking and pre-selecting. Remove the blanket and the fun begins. No rules and no limitations; it's first come, first served. Keep any items you like.

● Be sure children have a fair chance. Swaps involving children generally need a little more structure. Small children should be allowed to play with toys first; later, parents can help with selections.

● Provide tags or stickers for guests to mark their items. Sticky note paper works great.

● Remind guests to take what they want but use what they get.

● Donate leftover items to charity. This will keep everyone from dragging back more than they brought and will help keep a lot of closets clean.

Clothing

Creating and caring for a family wardrobe is a big job. And it's expensive. Shopping, washing, ironing, mending, lugging things to the dry cleaner . . . whew! It's enough to make you want to outfit everybody in polyester sweat suits. But if that's not an option, here are some great ideas to help.

Always test stain removal products on a hidden part of the garment to check for colorfastness and other problems.

STAIN REMOVAL

*S*tain removal may not be the most interesting topic in the world, but it certainly is necessary. The most important thing to remember is to act fast. There are lots of suggested remedies for various stains, but most can be treated with simple, inexpensive products you already have on hand. Here are some tips from the experts.

● Take immediate action. The longer a stain remains on the fabric, the more difficult it will be to get out.

● Always treat stains before laundering, even if it's just a little hand scrubbing with laundry detergent. A stain needs extra attention.

● Try to work from the underside of a garment to avoid grinding the stain through the fabric.

● Always use white towels and cloths to treat stains. Chemicals used to remove stains can cause color to bleed from one piece of fabric to another.

● Never use water and a grease solvent together. Allow water to evaporate completely before using another type of solvent.

● Never treat acetates or triacetates with acetone (found in nail polish remover), because it can dissolve these fabrics.

● Ammonia can change the color of some dyes. To restore the color, rinse the area with water, apply white vinegar, then rinse again with clear water.

● It's almost impossible to remove oil-based stains from durable or permanent-press fabrics, especially if they've been pressed or dried in the dryer.

- If one method of stain removal doesn't work, try another one. You can never be sure what will work on individual stains. Persistence can pay off.

Never use bleaches or bleaching solutions on delicate silks.

- Here are a few common stain removal techniques for washable fabrics:

ALCOHOLIC BEVERAGE
Soak immediately in cold water, then wash in warm, sudsy water. Rinse. If stain remains, you can soak silk, wool or colored items for half an hour in 2 tablespoons hydrogen peroxide mixed in a gallon of water. Launder. White linen, rayon, and cotton can be soaked in 1 tablespoon liquid chlorine bleach to each quart of water. Launder.

ANIMAL URINE
Soak in solution of 1 gallon warm water, 2 teaspoons dishwashing detergent and 4 tablespoons ammonia. Allow to soak for 30 minutes, then rinse. Soak in a solution of water and vinegar for about an hour. Rinse and air dry.

BLOOD
Sponge or soak in cold water for about 30 minutes. If stain remains, soak in lukewarm water and an enzyme presoak product, then launder.

CANDLE WAX
Firm up surface wax by rubbing with an ice cube, then scrape off with a knife. Place a clean towel underneath and wet thoroughly with grease solvent. Air dry, then launder as usual. Sometimes a colored candle will leave a dye stain as well. After treating for the wax stains, if the fabric is bleachable, soak in a solution of water and chlorine bleach. Launder.

Never iron or dryer-dry stained fabrics. Heat causes many stains to become permanent.

CHEWING GUM

Chill with ice cube, scrape off with knife or spoon. Treat with grease solvent. Launder as directed.

CHOCOLATE

Sponge or soak in cool water for half an hour. Work full strength detergent or soap into stain. If the stain also contains milk, soak in warm water and an enzyme laundry product, then launder.

COFFEE

Try soaking or dabbing with a solution of water, ammonia and soap. Then flush with hot water. Older stains can be treated with glycerin (available at drug stores.)

CRAYON

Machine wash in hot water using laundry soap and 1 cup baking soda. If color remains, launder again in hottest water that is safe for the fabric, and bleach, if safe.

DEODORANT

Place stain face down on cloth, sponge back of stain with a grease solvent. Allow to dry, then rub with full strength liquid detergent. Launder in hottest water safe for fabric.

FRUIT OR BERRY

Sponge with a solution of 1/2 tablespoon salt and 2 1/2 cups of cold water. If safe for fabric, pour boiling water through the stain. Apply soap or detergent directly to the stained area and launder. Or, soak in an enzyme laundry product, then launder.

GRASS

Sponge with alcohol or non-oily fingernail polish remover. Work liquid detergent into stain, then rinse and air dry.

GREASE OR TAR

Place stained area face down on a towel. Pour grease solvent through stain and allow to air dry. Rub with liquid detergent, rinse, and launder. Fresh grease stains can also be treated by covering the spot with cornstarch for 24 hours, which allows the powder to absorb the grease.

INK

Place a blotter under the fabric. Drip a grease solvent through the spot, and soak in a solution of soap and warm water. Rinse in cold water. (Some ink cannot be removed.)

KETCHUP

Soak in an enzyme detergent, then launder.

LIPSTICK

Wash immediately with cold saltwater or vinegar solution. You can also dissolve set lipstick with glycerin. For tougher stains, try blotting with denatured alcohol or hydrogen peroxide. Then wash in an enzyme detergent.

MILDEW

Brush off as much as possible. Rub stain with liquid detergent, then launder. If stain remains, launder using a bleach that is safe for the fabric. (Sometimes serious mildew stains can cause permanent damage to fibers and are impossible to remove.)

MILK OR MILK PRODUCTS

Soak in cold water. Rub full-strength detergent or soap directly on the stain. Launder as directed. (You can also soak in warm water with an enzyme laundry product, then launder.)

Use products carefully. Many chemicals can be dangerous if used improperly.

MUSTARD

This stain can be tricky, so act fast. Scrape or brush any remaining mustard. Flush with grease solvent. If stain remains, saturate the fabric with hydrogen peroxide, then add a small drop of ammonia. Allow to sit for about 15 minutes. Rinse thoroughly and allow to dry. Launder as directed.

PAINT

Determine the type of paint. Blot with water or the type of solvent recommended as thinner on the label. Then apply soap or detergent directly to stain and work in. Launder as directed.

RESTAURANT EMERGENCY STAINS

Red wine stains can be neutralized with white wine or club soda. A quick dose of salt is excellent at removing ketchup, wine and other stains that need to be absorbed, and of course a napkin dabbed in ice water can be used as well.

SHOE POLISH

Sponge with rubbing alcohol, then launder in hot water.

WINE

First dab up all liquid. Generously blot fresh stains with club soda, and rinse with cool water.

CLOTHING EMERGENCIES

lothing emergencies can be a disaster at the office. Runway models deal with them every day, so here are a few of their tricks. Some of these ideas seem silly at first, but in an emergency most of us will try anything. Even a wacky idea is better than none at all.

Remove wine or ketchup spills by dumping salt on the stain. Rub gently while the salt absorbs the color, then rinse with cold water.

● Rubber bands will hold up sweater and jacket sleeves that are a little too long or just won't stay in place. Men can use them to keep socks from slipping down their ankles.

● A little tape inside the neck will prevent a makeup ring on a blouse if you have to wear it again.

● Models use hair spray for everything, including static cling. Be sure to spray only on the underside of fabrics.

● A spritz of hair spray can also stop a run in your pantyhose, in an emergency.

● Fix a run with a dab of bar soap.

● Of course, hair spray works to remove ballpoint ink stains. Just spray liberally and keep working with it.

● Make scruffy nails look a little cleaner and whiter by lightly scraping them over a white bar of soap. Then rub a little soap over the tops of your nails and buff with a tissue for shine.

● A stuck zipper can often be "lubricated" by rubbing both sides of the teeth with a lead pencil. The graphite will help it to slide.

● Dirty and dull shoes can be refreshed with a dab of hand lotion and a tissue.

You can also use glue to keep a lightweight blouse or shirt closed when you've lost a button. It can save you from embarrassing gaps.

● Sometimes a broken zipper can be fixed by pinning it together where the teeth have broken. Thread the tab back on above the broken spot and zip closed from there.

● Remove scuffs from shoes with an ordinary pencil eraser. This can also work on leather and suede clothing.

● White-out will cover any marks or spots on white belts, bags, shoes, or even fabric.

● Use a chunk of pencil eraser to replace the lost back on a pierced earring.

● Repair a burn hole or tear by snipping a small piece of fabric from the hem, then glue it to the garment underneath the hole. Be sure to trim any loose threads.

● Water-soluble glue will also hold a loose hem in place. Make sure it's water soluble so it can be cleaned later.

● Attach shank buttons with pins.

● Be prepared. Attach a safety pin to an inside seam of all your clothes, just in case.

● To make a little extra room in a too-snug waist, use a rubber band. Loop it though the button hole and over the button. This will keep your skirt or slacks in place and give you a little breathing room.

● Color your leg with a marker under a hole or snag in black or navy panty hose.

● Staple hems and seams that come loose. But be sure to fasten them with the smooth side in, so that the staple won't snag your stockings.

So, if finding a sewing kit at work is a little like looking for a needle in a haystack, try these few tips to camouflage a clothing crisis.

CLOTHING CARE

Clothing takes a large percentage of the family budget and should be considered an investment. Professional cleaning is the only way to care for certain items, but not for everything. Here are some tips to help you care for your family's wardrobe without spending a fortune on products and dry cleaners.

Protect canvas shoes from permanent stains by spraying them in advance with a spray fabric guard or regular spray starch.

● Read the clothing tag. Manufacturers usually have room for only one recommended cleaning method. If a tag says "dry-clean only," it means just that. But if it just says "dry-clean," other methods, such as hand washing, are often safe.

● Before hand washing any garment, be sure to do a washing test on an inconspicuous area.

● Sometimes the main part of a garment is washable, but the lining and interfacing are not. Be sure to test these areas carefully.

● Do your hand laundry in your washer. Just start the tub and add a little detergent. Use the soapy water for your hand washing, then rinse it under the water still flowing into the tub. By the time the tub is full, you should be finished with your hand washing, and the water will still be fine to add a regular load of laundry.

● Don't overfill your washing machine. Not only will it keep your clothes from getting clean, the agitation will cause them to pill and wear out faster.

A cup of vinegar added to the rinse cycle of your wash will cut the static attraction of lint to clothes.

● Lint can make clothing look old and worn, but much of it can be prevented by proper laundering. Lint is caused by an overfilled washer, not enough water to wash lint away, not enough detergent to hold lint in suspension, a dirty lint filter, or even too much bleach.

● Lint can be removed from certain fabrics by lightly rubbing with sand paper or lightly shaving with a disposable double-edged razor.

● To cut down on pilling, wash man-made fibers separately from terry cloth and other fabrics that tend to rub. Line-drying items that tend to pill will also help.

● Some clothing that has pilled can be improved by carefully rubbing with a pumice stone.

● Most hand-washed sweaters will have a better feel if you add a little fabric softener to the final rinse.

● Don't just lay a sweater flat to dry. The secret to a professional finish on a hand-washed sweater is a rolling pin. After washing and squeezing out excess water, lay the damp sweater on a clean towel and use the rolling pin to shape and flatten all seams and openings. This will avoid the puckering that can make a sweater look old and worn.

● Protect expensive ties by spraying them with a spray fabric guard before wearing.

● Body oils can discolor and ruin white shirt collars long before the shirt wears out. To prevent this, iron a little talcum powder or cornstarch into the collar before wearing to help absorb the oils, and they'll wash right out.

● You can also protect white collars on children's party clothes with the same products.

● Avoid what dry cleaners call "mystery stains." Never get dressed until all antiperspirants, perfumes, and lotions are dry. These often show up later as stains on your best clothing.

LIFE EXPECTANCY OF CLOTHES

With proper care, here's how long the experts say you can expect your clothes to last.

Wool and blend suit	*4 years*
Lightweight suit	*2 years*
Cloth coat	*3 years*
Leather coat	*4 years*
Cotton and blend shirt	*2-3 years*
Sweater	*4 years*
Daytime dress	*2 years*
Evening dress	*3 years*

Buy shoes with chunkier heels. They tend to resist the scratches and nicks that can ruin slender heels.

DRESSING DOWN

*A*s women have become comfortable with their roles in the work place, they've become uncomfortable with the demands on their wardrobe. Dressing well for work is a significant cost of doing business, and women are looking for ways to cut back. Instead of buying cheaper clothes, they've found some clever ways to make nice things go further. They're still dressing for success, but they've put their foot down at excessive spending. Here are some of the best ideas to cut through the fashion fray.

● Try to encourage your company to institute Free Dress Day, usually Fridays, where everyone is permitted to "dress down" in casual clothes. This eliminates the need for one expensive outfit each week.

● Plan when and where you'll dress in your best clothes.

● Schedule all important meetings on one or two days, then dress in your best, most professional outfits.

● Understand your corporate culture. The term "corporate casual" is a few steps below a suit and silk blouse, but it doesn't mean jeans and a tee shirt. Too casual a look can be a career disaster.

● Choose dresses over more expensive suits. A nice dress can be less expensive and less hassle for work days. Experts emphasize that dresses are a good choice if they're tailored and conservative—no lace collars or other distinctly feminine details.

● Select clothes in all-season fabrics that can be worn nearly year round.

● Try to select things that you can wash yourself. Dry cleaning isn't just expensive, it's a hassle.

● Don't waste money on coordinating shoes. A few basic pumps in neutral colors will look good with everything.

● Spend your money on things you wear everyday. A good watch, handbag, and coat go a long way to adding polish.

● Spend more on solid-color items, less on prints. Prints tend to be more obvious, so you can wear them less often, and a print fabric can look dated long before it wears out.

● Protect your good clothes from obvious signs of wear—especially collars and cuffs. These areas tend to wear out first.

● Prevent tears and snags in blazer lining by putting on rings, watches, and other jewelry after you've slipped into your jacket.

● Never carry pens, keys, or other heavy objects in pockets. They can cause stains and rips, and they also tend to pull the fabric out of shape, causing the garment to look old.

● Alternate how you wear your jacket sleeves. Roll them up from time to time to avoid frayed and worn cuffs.

● Wear scarves or high-neck blouses, especially with lighter-colored jackets. When a neckline is in direct contact with your skin, friction and body oils will stain and fray the collar.

● Try to step into clothes rather than pull them over your head. Brushing against your face can leave a makeup stain. Models put a silk scarf over their head before they pull on clothes.

Allow perfumes, deodorants, and lotions to dry completely before getting dressed. These things can stain your clothes.

Don't wash clothes too often. The friction of washing, even hand washing, causes clothes to look old.

● Don't dry-clean too often. Experts say that most garments can withstand no more than 20 or 30 dry cleanings. It's hard on fabric.

● Let your clothes air out after wearing. Never put them directly in the closet at the end of the day. You'll probably have to clean them less often.

● Try to wear the same pins on jackets. Not only will it leave holes in an obvious part of a garment, jewelry can sometimes leave spots and discolorations that cannot be removed.

I R O N I N G

*S*ure, it's not a pressing problem, but statistics show that people are spending less money at professional cleaners and doing more of their own ironing and pressing. And no wonder. Doing the job yourself can save a couple of dollars per item. So here are a few hot tips.

Buy an iron with a treated soleplate. Like a nonstick fry pan, the surface is protected to keep it clean and smooth.

● Consider buying a new iron. New features make today's irons more user friendly.

● Look for a type of drip-stop system. Better heat control prevents the steam from spitting and spotting clothes.

● This system also prevents those nasty little brown spots that spit from your iron. It's not rust, by the way, but rather tiny lint balls that have been trapped, and more or less cooked, by your iron.

● Look for a continuous-steam feature. This Cadillac of features uses a large water tank that actually boils the water to create a continuous steam release.

● Select an automatic shut-off. It's a safety feature that automatically turns the appliance off if it's been idle for a period of time. This is perfect for the person who leaves the house and immediately wonders if the iron is turned off.

● Look for an adjustable cord. This is usually mounted in the center rear, and adjusts to various ironing positions, including left-handed use.

● Check out the button groove. This is the little indentation around the front of the iron. It's designed to help you get a smooth, professional look by allowing you to press easily around buttons. The best ones will run the entire length of the iron.

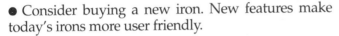

● Consider a spray-mist or burst-of-steam feature. This is the best solution for fabrics with persistent wrinkles. A powerful burst of steam can tame even the toughest linen collar.

● Once you've selected your iron, here's how to get the most out of it:

Understand the difference between pressing and ironing. When instructions say to press a garment, lift and lower the iron to the fabric. Ironing means that you glide the iron over the fabric.

Knits and other delicate fabrics should be pressed rather than ironed.

Use a pressing cloth when ironing fragile fabrics. The extra layer of light cloth will keep the garment clean and prevent scorching.

Before using a steam-burst feature, be sure the fabric will not spot. Silks are especially prone to water spotting.

Never iron over a stain because that will set it. If you absolutely must wear something with a spot, just iron around it.

Always lift the iron to allow steam to escape from under it. The heat and steam buildup can harm fabrics. And never press wool while steam is still rising from the garment.

To steam very delicate items like silk ties, wrap a steam iron with a damp cloth and hold it near the garment until wrinkles are eased out.

CLOTHING STORAGE

A change of weather usually means a change of wardrobe. Packing clothes away for the season requires a little care to make sure they'll be in good shape to wear again next year. Here are a few great tips to help you safely store seasonal clothing.

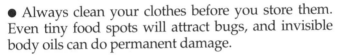

Rinse out all starch. It's corrosive to fibers and it's a favorite food for bugs.

● Always clean your clothes before you store them. Even tiny food spots will attract bugs, and invisible body oils can do permanent damage.

● Rinse everything twice. Detergent left in clothes can cause chemical changes in the fabric.

● Wash everything in soft water. Hard water can cause yellowing and rust spots. (See Water Softness Test on next page)

● Never put clothes in plastic. Polyethylene bags, like the kind you get from the dry cleaner, can emit a gas that can alter some dyes.

● Use mothballs in a closed, vented container like a coffee can punched full of holes. The vapors are heavier than air, so always place them above your clothes so they can filter down through the closet.

● Never use mothballs with plastic bags or wrapping. Mothballs can cause plastic to become sticky and damage fabrics.

● Because plastic is airtight and clothes really need to breathe, it's best to store all clothing in fabric or paper.

● Old sheets and pillowcases are perfect containers for storing clothes.

Always use padded hangers. To make your own, fasten old shoulder pads to a regular coat hanger.

● To make a jacket-sized garment bag, just cut a hole at the top of a pillowcase and slip it over a hanger.

● To make a larger bag, use a stapler to fasten sheets into the perfect size.

● Never carpet your closets. Carpet attracts dust and other debris that attracts the kind of bugs that love to eat fabric.

WATER SOFTNESS TEST

In a glass jar, combine two cups hot water with one teaspoon laundry detergent. Shake vigorously. Soft water will have a lot of sudsing action and the bubbles will last for a few minutes. Hard water will have only a few bubbles and they will disappear quickly.

Clothing

JEWELRY CLEANING

*W*e really don't think about it much, but jewelry is an expensive part of our wardrobe. Most of us have a few nice things and a bigger collection of less expensive costume pieces. They all need to be cleaned and stored properly. Here's what you need to know.

Store costume jewelry in a drawer filled with inexpensive dividers. Line them with pieces of soft cloth to prevent scratches.

● First, start with proper storage. Keep your best pieces in a lined jewelry box. They'll be protected from dust and scratches.

● Store earrings in old ice cube trays or egg cartons. Tuck a small piece of cotton or cloth on the bottom of each section.

● It's important to keep necklaces and chains from tangling, because it's often impossible to straighten them again. A simple trick is to slip them into a length of soda straw, then clasp the two ends together. Cut the straw a little shorter than half the length of the necklace or bracelet.

● Line a small drawer or box with a piece of styrofoam. Store pierced earrings by poking them into the foam. Drop earring backs into a small box.

● Have good jewelry checked by a professional once a year to be sure settings, strings, and clasps are in good condition.

● Clean your jewelry, especially the good stuff. Because it's worn so close to the body, it can collect body oils, lotions, and even tiny particles of skin. Not only does this dull the sparkle, but accumulated grime can settle into the prongs and compromise the setting.

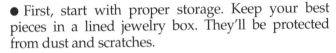

Clean leather watchbands with saddle soap or a leather cleaner.

● If you clean jewelry in the sink, be sure to keep the drain closed. Lay a soft washcloth on the bottom of the sink to prevent scratches and as double protection from gems slipping down the drain.

● Clean watchbands. Because we tend to wear them every day, they can get pretty nasty. Gold or stainless steel watchbands should be removed from the watch if possible, then soaked clean in a solution of water and sudsy ammonia.

● Pearls are like silver; they become more beautiful the more they're used.

● Pearl rings and pins can be soaked clean in mild soapy water. Rise and pat dry.

● It's best not to soak a pearl necklace in water because the string can get soaked, stretch, weaken, and even break. Instead, wash pearls with a cloth dipped in soapy water. Gently wipe pearls clean, then lay to dry on a soft towel.

● Pearls can be made more lustrous by gently wiping with a tiny drop of olive oil, then buffing with a soft flannel cloth.

● Gold chains should be soaked clean in a solution of water and sudsy ammonia. Soak for about 10 or 15 minutes, or until the water is dirty. Rinse and pat dry. Be very careful not to bend or tangle chains.

● Silver jewelry should be lightly buffed with a soft cloth after every wearing. It's important to remove fingerprints, because they can discolor the silver.

● Clean silver with a silver cloth or lightly rub with silver polish. To keep it looking good, you can store it in a pouch designed to protect silver tableware.

● You can also clean silver by rubbing gently with a bit of dry baking soda on a soft cloth.

● Diamonds should be soaked in a solution of warm water and sudsy ammonia. Gently brush the stone with a soft toothbrush to remove grime. Take care to clean near the prongs, because this is where most dirt collects.

Emeralds are very delicate and should be cleaned gently. Lightly swish the piece in soapy water, rinse and pat dry.

● Sapphires can be soaked in water and ammonia, then brushed lightly with a toothbrush, rinsed, and patted dry.

● Other jewelry should be carefully washed in gentle soap and water, then completely dried.

● To be sure nooks and crannies are dry, place jewelry on a towel and gently dry with your hairdryer on the low setting. Be very careful not to allow the heat to disturb any setting, strings, or glue.

PANTY HOSE

On may 15th, 1940, the first nylon stockings went on sale. The stores were mobbed, and women haven't stopped buying them since. Panty hose account for a big chunk of the working woman's wardrobe, so here are a few tips to help stretch your stocking budget.

● Buy stockings with reinforced toes because they're less vulnerable to snags and holes in the toe area.

● Buy the largest size that will fit. Remember, the less stress on the fabric, the longer it will last.

● If you're between sizes, and most of your weight is below the waist, choose the larger size. If you're top heavy, the smaller size will probably be better.

● Consider buying support panty hose. Today's fibers make them very durable, while still being sheer and comfortable.

● Be sure to check fiber content. A small percentage of lycra or spandex usually improves durability.

● Buy panty hose in quantity on sale, or purchase slightly imperfect ones from a national catalog or special off-price store.

● Choose panty hose with a center panel rather than a center seam. They'll fit better and be a lot more comfortable.

● Removing jewelry and dampening your hands will help prevent snags when putting on hosiery.

● Fiber experts at a national company say that freezing panty hose for a longer life is just a myth.

● But, the same experts say that a final rinse in beer will help. It coats the fibers and helps them to last longer.

● Some experts also claim that a rinse in salt water will help, too. Use about a half cup of salt for each quart of water.

Clear nail polish is still the all-time favorite for stopping a run, but in an emergency you can use hair spray or a wet bar of soap.

FRENCH REWEAVING

French reweaving is an excellent way to repair sweaters and other damaged knits.

Don't throw out good clothing just because it's damaged. A serious tear or burn can be repaired by an old technique called "French reweaving." French reweaving is done by hand, using magnifying glasses and special needles. Reweavers actually pull threads from the garment itself, and weave them to match the damaged area. This means that even if the garment is old and faded, the repaired area can match perfectly.

● Even light chiffon can be made as good as new.

● Synthetic materials can also be repaired.

● Raincoats or other items made from treated fabrics can be repaired, but the reweaving may be slightly noticeable.

● The overall condition of the garment will determine if it can be repaired. If reweaving is impossible, ask for suggestions for a creative alteration. Sometimes they can add a pocket or design some other way to camouflage the hole.

● Sweaters that have been damaged by moths can often be completely restored.

Almost any type of fabric can be repaired, except for velvet and some very fine silks.

● Bleach stains or other fabric damage can also be corrected by removing the offending threads and reweaving the area.

● The process is ideal for men's suits that have cigarette burns or other small holes.

● French reweaving is precision handwork, and when done expertly can restore a damaged garment to perfect condition.

IF THE SHOE FITS

*T*hey say that "a shine on your shoes puts a smile on your face." If that's the case, you'll be smiling all the way to the bank, because taking care of your shoes is the most important thing you can do to extend the life of expensive footwear. Here are a few tips to make it easier.

Remove mild scuff marks from light-colored shoes with an art gum eraser, available in art supply stores.

● Cover deep nicks and scratches on navy shoes with a dark blue felt tip marker. If you need to cover a large scuff mark, test a small patch of the shoe before you start. Apply as many coats as needed to match shoe color.

● Salt stains from snowy winter streets can be removed with a solution of equal parts vinegar and water. Dab the mixture gently on the salt stain. Be careful not to saturate the leather, which could leave a water ring.

● To steam clean suede shoes at home, use a soft dry brush and a pot of boiling water. Gently brush the shoe, then hold it over the pot until the steam has raised the nap on the suede. Lightly brush again in one direction.

● Use fine sandpaper to remove scuff marks or water stains from suede shoes.

● Suede shoes can be keep looking fresh by rubbing with a dry sponge after each wearing.

● For a hot wax shine, carefully melt the top layer of a can of paste wax shoe polish until the wax forms a puddle. Apply the liquid wax with a soft cloth. Buff, then sprinkle lightly with water. This is what's known as the famous "spit shine." Buff again for a high gloss. Although this gives a great shine, too much hot waxing can cause leather to dry out.

One-liter plastic soda bottles make excellent boot trees to help keep leather boots in shape.

● Apply a light coat of petroleum jelly to shine up patent leather shoes. This is a great way to teach kids how to polish shoes, because it's simple and won't make a mess.

● Keep shoes in shape by using shoe trees or stuffing tissue paper into toes. It's especially important if they get wet, or even damp from sweating.

● New shoes will last longer if you have taps put on the toes before you wear them.

● Replace worn heels as soon as possible to avoid damage to the body of the shoe. Waiting too long can ruin the shoe.

● Polishing shoes regularly will help prevent scuffs and stains. Even a quick coat of polish will offer some protection.

● Liquid shoe polish is best for covering scuffs, while paste wax gives shoes the best shine.

● White toothpaste will remove scuffs from silver or gold shoes.

● Cover scuff marks on white shoes with white-out correction fluid, then polish.

● Badly scuffed shoes can be restored with a two-step treatment. First, apply a coat of liquid shoe polish, which covers scuffs more effectively. Use multiple coats if necessary. Once scuffs are covered, apply a coat of cake wax polish. Buff vigorously for the best shine.

● Driving will cause scuffs on heels. Generally you don't notice them, but they're visible to everyone when you walk away. Prevent this by keeping a folded washcloth as a heel rest on the floor of your car.

● Change shoes frequently. Try not to wear the same shoe all day long, and never wear them two days in a row. Just like your feet, they need to rest.

Money

"I have enough money to last for the rest of my life . . . provided I die next Thursday."

This statement pretty much sums up the way many of us feel about our money. But the experts say that the problem for most of us is not that we don't have enough money, but rather that we don't have enough knowledge about money. Maybe. Anyway, here are some of our most popular *Better Living* tips for squeezing a little more out of the old paycheck.

Figure out how much you'll really lose. On average, more than half of a second income is dedicated to work-related expenses.

LIVING ON A SINGLE INCOME

*R*esearch from the early '90s shows that 47% of families headed by a married couple rely on two sources of income. In about 26% of the cases, both spouses are holding down full-time jobs. But with the pressures of today's busy lifestyle, many families are taking a second look at the real value of two parents working.

For middle-income families, about 56% of the second earner's wages are consumed by work-related expenses. For upper-income families, that figure rises to 68%. Many are deciding that it's just not worth it.

Millions of families live successfully on a single income, but making a change can be difficult. Here are some tips to help make the transition a little smoother.

● Begin planning at least a year ahead. It will take that long to get savings and finances in order.

● Decide whether this is a permanent or temporary situation. Planning to live on one income for a few years is a lot different from planning to make the change forever.

● Begin paying off debts. Focus first on high-interest credit cards and try to be debt-free before you quit.

● Think about the psychological issues. Many people feel guilty about staying home while a spouse works. Money can become a real battleground for control.

● If you're considering refinancing your mortgage, do it now. It's easier to qualify for a loan with two incomes.

● Consider getting a home equity line of credit. It will be easier to qualify while you still have two incomes, and you might need the money in case of an emergency. It should be considered emergency money only, and never used for regular expenses.

● Build up an emergency savings fund. Try to accumulate enough money to pay your expenses for three months. This should be kept in an investment that is very safe, and is easily available should you need it.

● Don't scrimp on insurance. Living on one income makes you more vulnerable to financial problems in an emergency.

● Make sure the wage earner has disability insurance. It should be enough to replace about two-thirds of his or her salary.

Don't stop saving. Even though you may need to cut back for a while, you shouldn't stop saving altogether.

● Practice living on one income. Start using the main income to pay all the expenses that will continue and use the second income for work-related costs only. Then use what's left over to retire debt or build emergency savings. This will give you a feel for your new budget.

● Start cutting back on your lifestyle. One of the great shocks to couples who make the transition is discovering what little money is left over for luxuries. Get used to a simpler way of life before you're forced into it.

● Stop shopping. Shopping for recreation can be a bad habit that can lead to disaster when you cut back to a single paycheck.

● Plan how you'll spend your time. Some people find it difficult to live without the stimulation of the work place. Start organizing how you'll spend your day.

● Be realistic. Living on one income is possible only if you're willing to make the necessary lifestyle changes.

● Consider part-time work. If a single-income lifestyle is simply impossible, consider working part-time. Studies show that women who work part-time actually experience less stress than either women who work full-time in the work place or full-time in the home.

Money

BUILDING A NEST EGG

*I*f you think you don't make enough money to start saving, think about this. Financial planners tell story after story of working people who manage to start small, save regularly, and build a sizable nest egg to finance a comfortable retirement. Many even retire early with plenty of money stashed away for travel. The secret is to make saving a priority by adjusting the way money is spent day-to-day. Here are some basic tips to help you find the money to build your nest egg.

Know the difference between your wants and needs. Spend for things you need. Cut back on things you want.

● Start an automatic savings program. If your employer doesn't offer a direct savings deduction, have your bank automatically transfer a fixed amount from your checking account to a savings account.

● Live a bit below your means. The best way to build savings fast is to spend less and save the difference. Keep your car and major appliances an extra year, cut back on obvious luxuries, and scale down your lifestyle.

● Cut flexible expenses by 2%, then build up to more. Almost anybody can achieve the 2% goal with very little sacrifice. Cut back on wardrobe expenses, eliminate expensive hobbies, trim automobile costs, and buy a little less at the grocery store.

● Cut back on regular discretionary spending. Drink water instead of vending machine sodas, brown bag your lunch, borrow books and videos from the library, and do your own ironing and other household chores. Because these are not one-time expenditures, the savings will add up all year long.

Stop using credit cards. Keep one for emergencies and put it away. Continue to pay off any existing charges and stop using it for day-to-day expenses.

● Cut back on impulse spending. For most people, browsing through stores for recreation is an expensive practice. Try to cut back on visits to stores and malls. If you do go, leave your checkbook and credit cards at home.

● Trim household expenses. Cut power bills by using less energy, compare insurance costs for lowest rates, set a fixed amount for cleaning products, cut back long distance calls, and eliminate premium cable channels.

● Or use the two credit card technique. Get one card with a low interest rate (this will most likely require an annual fee) and use that for any large emergency purchases you'll have to pay off over time. Get a second card that has no annual fee (this one will most likely have a higher interest rate), and use it for small purchases that you will pay off every month.

LOW-COST CAREERS

The cost of a four-year college degree is now several thousand dollars and is simply out of reach for many people. In addition, many working adults who desire a college degree cannot devote the time necessary to complete the work. Why not consider one of the many alternatives that require a much smaller investment of time or money? Here are a few ideas.

Ask about "telecourses." These video classes allow you to earn credits without having to attend regular classes.

● Instead of investing four years at an expensive college, take the basics at a community college where costs can be much lower per credit hour. Then transfer credits to finish up.

● Look for colleges that offer a degree in three years. These programs are designed to help students save time and money.

● Look for courses "on line." Some schools offer credit for courses that you take via computer. They can be less expensive and allow you to work at your own pace.

● Ask about earning credit for what you've learned in life. Many colleges will allow you to "test out" of certain courses if you have related experience.

● Ask about internships. Many schools will offer credit for on-the-job experience you acquire as an intern in your chosen field. Internships are usually for the duration of a semester and can be paid or unpaid.

● Ask your company about tuition reimbursement. Often companies will reimburse employees for costs related to furthering their education in a job-related field.

● Check out scholarships and grants. The library is full of books that will explain how you can apply for the millions of dollars available to students of nearly every age, income level, and academic standing.

● Think about training up. Learn a basic trade at a technical school and use that to get a job at a company that will pick up the tab for more education. This way you can earn while you learn.

● Consider a career that requires less time and money for training. Paralegal assistance, court reporting, medical technology, building trades, and cosmetology are only some of the examples that offer good opportunities.

Give Me Credit

*C*redit costs money. Like anything else you spend your money on, it can be a good investment or a bad one. Knowing when and how to use credit to your advantage is a great financial skill. Here are some tips from the experts.

When reasonable, try to use credit options that are tax deductible.

● Remember that the cheapest way to buy anything is to pay cash. Credit will always increase your costs. Be sure to factor this into your buying decision.

● Shop around for the best deal on credit in the same way you shop for the best deal on merchandise. This applies to credit cards as well as installment loans.

● As a general rule, the best way to use credit is to make the largest down payment you can, and pay off the loan in the shortest amount of time possible.

● Pay off one major installment debt before you take on another one. For example, a two-car family should try to have only one car payment at a time.

● If you can't afford cash for a luxury item, you probably can't afford credit. Remember that credit allows you to use things as you pay for them, but it cannot increase your standard of living.

● Try to pay off credit cards regularly—if not every month, then at least every so often. A revolving account can easily become permanent debt that will continue to grow.

● Don't charge anything that will not hold its value longer than the payments. Value can be assessed in money, usefulness, or enjoyment.

● Make sure your payments are all nearly equal, especially the last one. Some loans are set up with a balloon payment—a very large payment at the end.

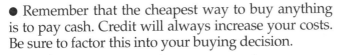

● Don't allow a credit contract to prevent you from saving. A regular savings plan, no matter how small, is a good sign on your credit report. And a nest egg is even more important when you have debts.

● How much can you borrow? One rule of thumb says that, excluding your mortgage, you should never owe more than 20% of your yearly after-tax income. For example, if your take home pay is $2000 a month, your maximum debt at any one time should be no more than $4,800. But remember, the less debt the better.

REFINANCING

*N*o matter how long you've owned your home, if you are still paying on the mortgage, it's a good idea to keep an eye on the interest rates. Rates can change, and with the simple act of refinancing you can save thousands of dollars. Even if you've refinanced your original mortgage, it can pay to refinance again. But don't stop there.

Try to refinance with your current mortgage company. It's possible some costs can be avoided.

● How much can you expect to save? Here's an example of a 30-year, $100,000 mortgage at 10%. Monthly payments for principal and interest are about $877. Refinance at 8%, and your payments drop to $733 a month. That's a savings of $144 every month.

● Here's the real money magic. Instead of allowing that extra money to slip away, you should invest it. In 10 years, at 10%, your $144 a month will grow to more than $25,000. If you invest it over the entire life of the mortgage—that's 30 years—you'll end up with a whopping $325,000!

● Refinancing can be a great idea, but it costs a little money up front. To refinance, you'll probably have to pay points, or a percentage of the loan, title search, and other fees. But often, these fees can be financed in the mortgage.

● Here's what you need to know to get started. If you plan to move in 2 to 5 years, you may be better off to keep your existing mortgage.

● Consider including the refinancing charges in the mortgage.

Shop around. Refinancing costs can differ as much as mortgage rates.

● Make sure your monthly savings will offset your closing costs in 1 to 3 years.

Check on
regulations. Some
cities require a
permit and limit
the number of
garage sales you
can have in one
year.

MAKING MONEY
WITH A GARAGE SALE

*T*urning trash into cash is the general idea behind most garage sales, and it seems to be working. According to one expert, the average garage sale these days nets about $250. So if making a little extra money sounds like a good idea, here's what you need to know.

● Try to go in with other families. The more merchandise you can offer, the better. To keep things straight, have each family tag their merchandise with a different-colored price tag.

● Advertise. Consider placing ads in a shopper's guide the week leading up to your sale, and in the local newspaper the weekend of the event.

● Organize your merchandise. For example, put household items in one area, toys in another. This will make it easy for people to find things, and will encourage them to consider other items.

● Use free advertising, too. Don't forget to post notices on public bulletin boards in stores and churches.

● Make sure everything looks clean. A few extra minutes shining up an old appliance can net you several extra dollars.

● Launder and press clothing. Kid's clothes can be big sellers if they look good, but they can end up in the trash if they look wrinkled and messy.

● Make sure you have plenty of change. Keep some coins in a change box, but keep the bulk of your money safely in a waist pack that you wear the entire day.

● Have an extension cord set up for people to try electrical items, and keep a tape measure handy for them to measure larger items.

Don't negotiate until the afternoon. Stick to your original prices throughout the morning, and be willing to bargain after about one o'clock.

● Be honest about the condition of items. If something doesn't work, say so. Just because it's broken doesn't mean people won't buy it.

● Set up a temporary dressing area with a mirror for trying on clothes. It can be in your garage, or even sheets hung over the clothesline.

● Place a couple of large, interesting items near the street to attract attention as people drive by. Don't move them once they're sold, just tag them.

● Organize small items by price. Use boxes or baskets to hold lots of 10- and 25-cent items.

● Price larger items individually. A rule of thumb says that items will sell for 20% to 50% of retail value, depending on condition. Adult clothing is worth about 10% of retail, and children's clothing a little more.

● Price things to sell. You don't want to give them away, but shoppers are more likely to buy several items if they believe things are bargain-priced.

● Keep your doors locked. Clever burglars have been known to distract homeowners at a garage sale while an accomplice slips into the house to remove valuables. No one thinks twice when they walk out of the house with a TV. They blend in with other shoppers.

● Never allow anyone to use your bathroom or phone. It's just not safe.

● Make browsing pleasant. The longer people stay, the more they are likely to buy.

● Donate leftover items to charity. You can make arrangements in advance for a charitable organization to pick up items at the end of the day. At least you'll get a tax deduction.

Instead of buying your lunch, brown bag just once a week. You'll save at least $3, or $150 a year.

HIDDEN MONEY

*W*ouldn't it be great to find a $1,000 that you've hidden away and forgotten about? Most of us have hidden money in our budgets—small change that we throw away on things we could do without. Finding these bits of hidden cash and putting them together in one lump sum is the trick. Lots of people have managed to scrape together hidden money for trips and other luxuries just by pinching pennies. Here are some suggestions for finding your hidden money.

● Skip the morning convenience store coffee habit. By brewing your own at home, you can save a couple hundred dollars a year. Double that for two people.

● Save your pocket change. Keep a jar on your dresser and drop your change in every night. One survey showed that people carry around an average of $1.28 in change. If you saved that much every work day, in one year you'd have about $334.

● Use the library. Figuring just two paperbacks and two video rentals a month, you can save well over $200 a year.

● Use coupons at the grocery and save 7% to 10% on your grocery bill. Add the savings to your hidden money fund.

● Reuse everything possible. Foil, gift wrap, ribbons, jars, plastic bags—saving the cost of replacing these things is another bit of hidden money.

● Avoid clothing that requires dry cleaning. It's like being forced to pay $5 every time you want to wear your outfit. Make it a point to buy clothing you can clean yourself.

● Cut back on the amount of personal and household products you use. Most people use way too much shampoo, dishwashing liquid, laundry detergent, cleaning agents, furniture polish, and other things. For example, instead of using a quarter size drop of shampoo, start with a dime size amount—you can always add more. Start with less, add if you need to. It's better for the environment and can add up in savings.

Don't buy checks from your bank. Checks from mail-order companies are much cheaper.

● Cut back on eating out. Remember, you're not just paying for the food: the tip, tax, and travel add about another 25% to the cost of the meal. That means out of every $10 you spend in a restaurant, $2.50 is essentially hidden money.

● Write instead of call. Talk is not cheap when you're paying long distance rates. Send a letter instead.

● If letters are out of the question, consider keeping in touch via computer. "On-line" communication can be less expensive and more fun than phone calls.

● Don't keep too much money in your checking account. It's best to keep any extra money in an interest-bearing account.

● Switch to lower-cost cosmetics. The extra cost associated with top-of-the-line cosmetics is for the elaborate packaging, advertising and all those "free" gifts with purchase. Less expensive products are not much different in actual quality.

● Buy generic drugs and toiletries, which can be about 50% cheaper than name brands. Because personal products are things you use every day, the savings can add up significantly over a year.

● Cut down on impulse items like gum, trinkets, kitchen gadgets, and small purchases on sale. This money can add up to a small fortune in useless spending.

Don't use your ATM unless it's necessary. Most banks charge a fee for the service.

● Consume a little less energy. Simply using the well-known strategies for cutting down at home and in your car can result in significant savings for most people. Think about what that means. In one month your electric bill could be $10 less, your water bill could be $2 less, the cost of gas for your car could be $8 less—that's $20 in hidden money. Over one year's time that can mean $240 in your pocket.

● Shop for sales on all significant purchases. It's a good idea to have a rule—never buy anything over $100 unless it's on sale. When you find the item you want, ask when it will go on sale. Most stores will be glad to let you know. Then be patient.

● Add up these small savings and you might be surprised at how much hidden money you can recover just by looking around.

MONEY MANAGEMENT

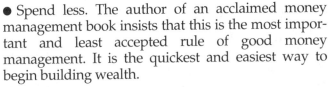y now, all the media hype about money management has made most of us feel completely confused and doomed to financial failure. Actually, there are no more geniuses in the financial world than there are anyplace else. The old question "If you're so smart, why aren't you rich?" really applies to a lot of the so-called experts trying to give us advice. As in most matters, the best advice is to educate yourself, then find a reliable expert to work with you. Here are some things you need to know.

Pay off debts. Any debt, including credit cards, eats away at personal wealth.

● Spend less. The author of an acclaimed money management book insists that this is the most important and least accepted rule of good money management. It is the quickest and easiest way to begin building wealth.

● Begin by saving a percentage of your income. Start where you can and try to build up to 15% to 20% of your pre-tax paycheck.

● Take advantage of tax-deferred savings plans first. The now popular 401K and other plans allow you the maximum savings advantage.

● Buy a home. Nearly everyone can benefit from home ownership. It can serve as shelter, a tax advantage, and a way to accumulate wealth.

● Manage your risk. Don't take the chance of compounding bad luck by being under-insured.

● Try not to overspend on financial services. Before you do business with any financial expert, make sure you understand how that person makes his or her money.

Diversify. This is for everybody, not just big investors.

● Build an emergency fund. Most experts recommend that before you develop any long-term investments, you should have in an easily accessible account enough money to cover two to three months of expenses.

● Be consistent. You may not be able to save much, but even a dollar a day, invested at 8% compounded interest, can add up to $5,595 in 10 years.

● Consider a consultation with a Certified Financial Planner to discuss your options and develop a financial strategy. Many planners will work for a flat fee rather than relying on commissions from investments they sell you.

● Ask about automatic dividend reinvestment plans. If you own stocks directly, many larger companies will allow you to reinvest your dividend in additional shares of stock without paying any fees or service charges.

● If you plan to invest in U.S. Treasury securities, consider the Treasury Direct program. It allows you to purchase U.S. Treasury bills, notes and bonds without paying a transaction fee to a broker. Write to the Bureau of Public Debt, Washington D.C. 20239, and ask to set up a Treasury Direct account. You'll receive forms that will allow you to purchase any new treasury offering.

● Plan for inflation. Estimate the present dollar cost for your goals, then calculate for inflation based on the number of years before you'll actually need the money. For example, using an inflation rate of 5%, a $10,000 dream vacation will probably cost about $26,500, 20 years from now.

● A couple of smaller investments in different areas is a safer plan than a single large investment in one place. One expert recommends not more than 10% of your money in any single investment.

● Where should you keep your savings? Only you can make that decision, but many experts agree on the basics of this plan:

Consider a discount broker. These companies offer similar services for lower fees. But remember, it's still important to make your own decisions.

B A S I C   M O N E Y   P L A N

Emergency money, equal to a minimum of three months' expenses, should be kept in a safe investment that allows you easy access to your money, such as a bank or money market mutual fund.

Savings for specific expenses that you will incur within four years or so should be kept in savings bonds, certificates of deposit, or some similar investment.

Savings that won't be needed for five years or more can be in slightly more aggressive investments, such as stock or bond mutual funds.

AVOIDING COMMON
MONEY MISTAKES

They say a fool and his money are soon parted, and that applies to most of us—at least once or twice. Every year we read about some rich and famous celebrity who, instead of having financial security, ends up broke. That person's unfortunate fate is usually due to one of a few common money mistakes.

Avoiding major financial errors, the kind that can affect the way we live, is a key to financial security. According to the experts, here's how to steer clear of life's most common money mistakes.

YOUNG ADULTS

● Don't skip health insurance. Young people think they'll never get sick. But the fact is, if they do become ill, it's much more likely to be serious and costly.

● Don't skimp on life insurance. Because young people are more likely to have more debts and young children, it's important to have adequate coverage. Term insurance is generally the cheapest and best way to have adequate coverage.

● Get renter's insurance. A lot of young people mistakenly believe that the landlord is responsible for everything. The fact is, you could lose all of your possessions in a fire or burglary and literally end up with nothing.

● Start saving 10% of your gross income. The cost of waiting to begin saving can dramatically reduce the amount of money you can accumulate in your lifetime.

● Pay off credit card debt. Young people are more likely to accumulate debt than are other age groups. Cars, credit cards, and college loans can quickly sink a person deep in debt, and climbing back out wastes valuable time and money. Even if you manage to become debt free, you'll always be behind where you could have been if you'd been more careful.

● Take advantage of retirement savings plans. It's hard for young people to think that far ahead, but starting early is one of the most important things you can do to help build financial security.

MIDDLE AGE

● Don't touch retirement money. At this age, many people have accumulated a nest egg, often in a retirement plan. It's very tempting to want to tap into the account to pay for a boat, a wedding or some other of life's expenses. It can be more costly than you might imagine. Taxes and penalties alone can cut your nest egg by up to 50%.

● Don't stop saving. Heavy expenses at this age often tempt people to cut back on saving. Remember, the more you save, the more you'll have available if you incur a genuine emergency.

● Plan for inflation. Estimates of your monthly income from pension and social security can be misleading. By the time you retire, you may easily need more than double your current income. Many experts believe that inflation is the greatest risk to financial security.

● Check out your financial advisor. Call professional organizations, ask for references and check them out; and be sure you understand how your advisor makes his or her money. Many people have been sold weak investments because their so-called "advisor" could make big commissions on them.

● Keep track of your investments—don't rely on someone else to do that for you. It's a hassle to stay on top of things, but there are thousands of sad stories about trusting people who lost everything because they relied on someone else to look out for them.

● Don't invest in something you don't understand. At best you'll always have a vague sense of worry, and at the worst you could lose everything through ignorance.

● Don't hold too much stock in the company you work for. It's too risky to have a significant portion of your savings, as well as your major source of income, in the same company. When you receive company stock, develop a solid plan to diversify.

● Make sure you have adequate liability coverage. An additional umbrella policy that covers injuries in your home and auto is relatively inexpensive, and can save you from losing everything.

SENIOR YEARS

● Don't be too conservative. Most people past 60 are more comfortable with less risky investments. While your overall financial plan should be more conservative, it's important to keep a portion of it in investments that can offer an opportunity for growth.

● Plan for a long retirement. Experts say that most seniors underestimate how long they're likely to live, and that can affect decision making.

● Watch out for scams. Older people tend to have accumulated the most money, so they are the prime targets for scams. Con artists have become very sophisticated, often suggesting an affiliation with churches, ethnic groups and other organizations. Scrutinize every investment and check out every single organization.

● Don't make investment decisions over the phone. Telemarketing schemes bilk unsuspecting Americans out of billions. If you're interested, write down the information, then say you'll call back after you check things out.

● Never give out personal information over the phone unless you made the call yourself. Do not reveal your checking account number, credit card information, or anything else, unless you know the person you're talking with, and are sure that he or she has a legitimate need for the information.

● Retirement communities should be carefully researched. Remember that states that have no income tax make up the income in other ways: high property and sales taxes, for example.

● Make sure you understand the tax liability associated with your pension. If you retire to another state, it's possible you will owe taxes to the state in which you earned your pension.

● Make sure your will is up-to-date. Careful planning can help to make sure your heirs—not the government—end up with the bulk of your estate.

● Be sure to arrange for a durable power of attorney. Should you become incompetent, you'll need a trusted person to make important decisions. You should also include your wishes regarding health care, often in the form of a living will, and make clear what life-support measures you consider acceptable.

Check your food at a drive-through. Fast food restaurants are notorious for forgetting to include something in an order. Just take a minute for a quick check.

GET WHAT YOU PAY FOR

One of the most basic secrets to good money management is to get what you pay for. Each year we foolishly give away millions of dollars for products that break, things we don't like, and merchandise we don't even receive. Here are some reminders to help you get what you pay for.

● Save all merchandise receipts for a year. Just stash them in a box, then if the product develops a flaw, you can still return it.

● Don't remove tags from clothes until just before you wear them. It's possible you'll change you mind or discover something wrong.

● Fill out and save warranties. It always seems so unimportant when you're opening a new product. But when something goes wrong, you want to be sure the company pays to fix it, not you.

● Take things back, even if you've kept them a long time. Some stores will say "no," but many will take things back with no questions asked.

● Watch at the grocery checkout to be sure all your groceries are packed and every bag is placed in your cart. It's easy to get distracted and forget something.

● Keep grocery receipts in a separate place for at least a month. You may need to return a product that turns out to be unsatisfactory.

● Have a complaint plan. Make copies of a generic complaint letter, leaving room to describe the product and the problem. This will make it a lot easier to write to manufacturers about defects. Some companies will not only refund your money, but will include valuable coupons as an apology.

WASTE NOT, WANT NOT

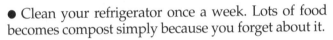t's estimated that American families waste at least 10% of their food, and that means 10% of their food budget. This includes household products such as toothpaste and shampoo. If your family is guilty of wasting too much, here are a few ideas to help prevent 10% of your food budget from going down the drain.

Measure everything. Studies show that cooks who guesstimate inevitably over measure.

● Clean your refrigerator once a week. Lots of food becomes compost simply because you forget about it.

● It's easy to deal with major leftovers. But a lot of waste occurs when we toss away lots of bits and pieces of good food.

● Don't let fresh fruit become overripe and go to waste. Chop it up and freeze it in a single container you keep in the freezer. When you have enough, you can whip up a mixed fruit pie or cobbler.

● Save small leftovers in simple ways. For example, leftover bits of meat and vegetables can be frozen and stored until the next time you serve pizza. Buy a plain pizza crust, top with the leftover toppings, and bake.

● Most salad vegetables spoil because people don't have time to prepare them. Instead of making a single salad, chop and prepare a whole bag of vegetables at once. You're more likely to eat the food if it's all ready to serve.

● Store bread and other baked goods in the freezer and remove only what you'll need.

● Never throw anything away until it's spoiled. Even if it's a small amount, you may find a use for it.

Use only reclosable drinks. Individual soda cans and juice packs are an invitation to waste.

● Measuring laundry products is another way to save. Only use the amount for the size load you are doing. Most package recommendations are appropriate for a large load. You only need about half as much for a small one.

● Water down things you tend to overuse. Dishwashing detergent and shampoo are great examples of this. Transfer the product to another bottle and add about 1/3 to 1/2 water.

● Attack the 10% waste problem by following the 10% rule. Try to buy and use 10% less of everything. Use 10% less coffee for brewing, 10% less toothpaste each morning, 10% less sugar in cooking, 10% less laundry detergent, and anything else you can think of.

● You can always adjust up or down, but with the 10% rule, most people only notice the difference in their grocery bill—a 10% savings.

Food

*E*ven for busy families who typically eat and run, there are times when food is the center of attention. We all know that homemade holiday treats are a part of childhood memories, that morning coffee is more like a deep breath than a beverage, and that a family dinner, prepared at home, is still a favorite way to celebrate special occasions. These next *Better Living* ideas are a collection of common sense advice and creative tips to help make quick work of kitchen chores.

Meat can be sliced more thinly when it is frozen first.

CLEVER CHEFS' SECRETS

oday's chefs are well known for their exotic and elaborate cooking methods, but they have a lot of clever cooking tips, too. Some come from the old-fashioned, European tradition of cooking, but many of today's professionals are geared to more modern concepts of quick and clever cooking techniques. But all of them reflect the professional desire to present food at its very best.

● Instead of salt and pepper shakers on the stove, fill a small bowl with a mixture of 3/4 salt and 1/4 pepper. It makes seasoning quicker and less messy.

● Always wash potatoes with cold water after slicing, to prevent any stickiness or off-taste from the cutting board or blade.

● Make excellent salad dressings by pouring oil and vinegar into the last bits left in bottles of mustard or ketchup. Shake and pour.

● The inner core of an onion can have a woody consistency, so be sure to trim it out before slicing or chopping.

● Instead of one large chopping board, it's better to use a few small ones. You won't have to transfer food to other containers before cooking, and you won't have to wash the board as you prepare different ingredients.

● To keep cutting boards in good condition, dry well after washing and then sprinkle with salt to help draw out moisture. Allow to sit, then treat with mineral oil.

● To keep plastic wrap from sticking to itself, store it in the refirgerator.

● Cut back on the salt in a recipe if the dish will bake for a long time. Slow cooking tends to bring out the salty taste in a dish.

Crush cloves of garlic in a zip lock bag to keep things neat and to keep your hands clean.

● Cut back on salt when cooking with wine. Wine tends to intensify the taste of salt.

● To delicately soften butter for cooking or spreading, cover with a heated pan while preparing other ingredients.

● For excellent flavor in a casserole or meat dish, create an old-fashioned baker's seal. Prepare the recipe in a crockery dish with a lid. Then make a thick dough from flour and water. Form the dough into a long thin roll and stick it around the rim of the dish. Place the lid on, pushing it into the dough to create a complete seal between lid and bowl. The food will be very tender and flavorful.

● Almost any dish that requires water, or boiling in water, can be improved by using broth or bouillon instead. Rice or potato dishes are good examples.

● Rice can be made in less time by preparing it like pasta. Just boil vigorously for about 10 minutes, uncovered. Drain and toss with butter.

● To get a professional look with steaks and chops, snip the fatty edges with kitchen scissors in three or four places before cooking. This will keep the meat from curling up during cooking.

● To improve flavor and texture, grate a raw potato into one pound of lean ground beef. This can be used for hamburgers, meatloaf, and other similar dishes.

● Instant potato flakes mixed in before cooking will also enhance the flavor of reduced-fat, ground beef.

● To remove the salty taste from ham, partially bake it, then drain off all juices. Pour a small bottle of ginger ale over the entire ham and return it to the oven until done.

A teaspoon of sugar will help peas to retain their color and flavor during cooking.

- Meat can be made more tender by soaking in vinegar and water for about 5 minutes. Then prepare as usual.

- Place lettuce leaves between slices of meat while reheating. This will prevent the slices from becoming dry and tough.

- Lay celery stalks in the bottom of a pan when roasting chicken or other meats. This will serve as a rack while adding moisture and flavor.

- Use thawed frozen spinach souffle for filling pasta or crepes.

- Store potato chips, crackers, and other crisp foods in the freezer during hot, humid weather. The humidity can cause them to become limp and tasteless.

- Parsley should be stored in a jar of cold water in the refrigerator. Just before adding it to a cooked recipe, it should be quickly rinsed in hot water to help release the flavor.

- When making salad dressing, prepare it ahead in the salad bowl, then store in the refrigerator. This will chill the bowl and dressing, as well as allow flavors to steep. Then, at meal time, place salad greens on top of the dressing and toss. Your salad will be crisp and perfect, and you'll only use one bowl.

- Use a muffin tin to bake apples, tomatoes, and stuffed peppers. It will prevent them from collapsing in the oven. You can buy microwave-safe tins as well.

- Gas burners are preferred by chefs because they can be more easily controlled. When cooking on an electric stove, you can accomplish the same thing by turning on two burners at once. Have one set high and the other set low. Then you can move your pan back and forth when you need to quickly change cooking temperatures.

● Refresh limp carrots and celery by covering them with cold water and ice cubes and allowing them to sit in the refrigerator.

● Rather than use diet margarines, make your own reduced-calorie butter.

B E T T E R   B U T T E R

1 pound softened butter
2 cups skim milk
1 envelope unflavored gelatin

Mix gelatin and 1 cup skim milk. Place over low heat until gelatin is dissolved. Blend in butter. Add the second cup of skim milk and mix throughly. Refrigerate.

When eating out, request that all meats be prepared well done.

FOOD SAFETY

oncerns over food safety have made everyone more aware of shopping for and storing food. Although our food supply is considered to be very safe, each year there are illnesses and deaths related to spoiled or contaminated food. While most grocers and food handlers are reliable, it's important to take the time to learn how to make good, safe choices.

● Check packages to be sure they're secure. Never buy a package that's dented, rusty or broken in any way.

● Never buy a brick pack that has become soft or flexible.

● Don't toss things into your cart. A lot of packages get damaged this way, which makes food vulnerable to contamination. Place them gently in the cart with heavy items on the bottom, more delicate items on top.

● Don't overbuy. Select only as much food as you can safely store. Many people are tempted to use outdated products because they want to avoid wasting food.

● Keep chicken away from everything else in your cart. A wet, leaking package can easily contaminate other foods with salmonella.

● Buy the freshest meat possible. Hamburger should be only one or two days old.

● Don't be fooled by the bloom on ground meat. It's perfectly normal for ground beef to be bright red on the outside and dark on the inside.

● Check liquid around hot dogs and luncheon meats. It should be clear.

Don't forget about pesticides. That's another reason to wash everything carefully.

● Most shrimp should be clean and pinkish white. Black spots beginning on the tiny swimmerettes can indicate age.

● Tap clam shells. If they're fresh, they'll close up.

● Don't buy green potatoes; they can be toxic. Any green should be cut away before cooking. And if there is a lot of green, the potato should be thrown out.

● Buy only enough eggs for two weeks and keep them stored in their carton. Refrigerator compartments are too warm.

● Make sure eggs are not stacked too high in the grocery store. The cartons on top may not be cool enough to stay fresh. To be safe, select from a lower level.

● Wash everything, including oranges and melons. Even if you remove the peel, dangerous contaminants can easily be transferred from the peel to the knife and onto the fruit.

● Clean your can opener. Regular cleaning with a solution of bleach and water is important.

● Make sure foods served to you are at a safe temperature. Cold foods should be cold; hot foods hot, not just warm.

● Remember that children, because of their smaller and more delicate bodies, are at a greater risk. Be very careful what and where you allow them to eat.

Herbs grow best in a sunny location. Tiny pots on your window sill will work fine.

HERBS

ooking with herbs is an important part of American cuisine and the key to healthy, low-fat recipes. And more and more, we're finding them useful for other things as well. A small herb garden in your back yard, or even on your window sill, can make herbs available all year long for free. Here are a few tips for growing and using herbs.

● Start simply. Decide on a few of your favorites and buy small plants from your garden center.

● Outdoors, grow them near your kitchen door. You'll be more likely to use them if they're easy to get to. Many herbs are simple and very inexpensive to grow from seeds.

● Dill grows quickly from seed. It can be snipped for cooking, and the seeds can be used for pickling.

● Parsley is easy to grow, but seeds should be soaked in water for 24 hours to speed up germination.

● Chervil is a little exotic, but it's simple to grow. Its flavor is similar to French tarragon.

● Sage is a good choice because it will flourish under most conditions. It's the main seasoning in most stuffing recipes and will make a welcome gift to friends at Thanksgiving.

● Chives are hardy and very useful in many recipes. Later in the growing season, they develop a pretty purple flower that can be used as a garnish.

● Incorporate herbs into your landscaping. Herbs like thyme and rosemary can grow into large, beautiful plants and will make your entire yard smell wonderful.

● Combine a few herbs for specific recipes in a single flower pot. For example, a "spaghetti pot" could contain oregano, basil, and chives.

Freeze extra herbs by chopping and storing in plastic freezer bags.

● Make herb butters by combining a stick of unsalted butter with 2 or more tablespoons of fresh herbs. Add a splash of lemon juice and blend (when using dried herbs you need less).

● Make your own poultry seasoning by combining savory, thyme, sage, and marjoram.

● Too much garlic in a recipe can be subdued by filling a tea ball with dried parsley. It will help absorb the flavor.

● Create homemade herb vinegars.

In a stainless steel pan, bring a good quality wine vinegar to a slow boil over moderate heat. Pour into sterilized bottles, then add a few fresh herbs of your choice. Store in a cool place for 2 weeks. It's best used within about 6 months.

● You can also make your own gourmet mustards with fresh herbs.

FRESH BASIL MUSTARD

4 tablespoons dry mustard
1 tablespoon white vinegar
2 tablespoons beer (room temperature)
1 clove garlic
1 teaspoon sugar
1 teaspoon salt
1/4 teaspoon turmeric
1 1/2 teaspoon chopped basil
2 teaspoons green pepper (finely chopped)
1/2 cup good quality olive oil

In a mixing bowl, use a wire whisk to combine mustard, vinegar, and beer. Blend thoroughly. Press garlic and add to mixture. Mix with sugar, salt, turmeric, basil, and pepper. Add oil gradually and blend till smooth.

Encourage kids to choose healthy snacks by making them more fun.

KIDS IN THE KITCHEN

Today's kids spend lots of time on their own in the kitchen. Busy schedules mean that even little ones need to know how to do the basics. Microwave ovens, new food technology, and helpful parents can make things a lot easier. So here are some great ideas to help junior cooks.

● Avoid sharp knives by teaching children to use a pizza cutter instead.

● Very young children can even use a pie server to cut things like soft fruits and sandwiches.

● Beware of steam burns from foods cooked in a microwave. Popcorn is a prime offender. Make sure kids open packages away from them and allow steam to escape slowly.

● Hollow out apples to use as cups for apple and other fruit juices. Kids get a kick out of drinking the juice, then eating the cup.

● Magically pre-slice bananas for cereal while the fruit is still in the skin. Here's the secret. Use a hat pin and push it through the banana skin at regular intervals on a seam. Just poke it in, then slide it back and forth until you feel it slice all the way through the banana. When you peel the banana, it will already be sliced. Kids will be amazed!

● Teach kids how to make their own fresh butter. You don't need a churn. Just pour about a cup of heavy cream into a clean pint jar. Close tightly and let kids begin to shake the contents. In about 30 minutes you have fresh, homemade butter. It makes a great gift for kids to take to special family dinners.

● Kids can make bite-sized snacks using their favorite crunchy crackers. Just top crackers with salsa and cheese for nacho snacks, and pizza sauce, cheese and pepperoni to create little crunchy pizzas. Then pop in the microwave for a few seconds.

Serve chunks of fresh fruit using a hollowed-out orange for the bowl.

● Serve kids snacks like raisins, nuts and trail mix in an ice cream cone. It's fun and they can eat the container.

● Two-tone sandwiches are fun. Use a cookie cutter and two kinds of bread to create your own bread puzzle. Just cut the same shape out of the center of two slices of bread, one dark, one light. Then switch the pieces—dark shape in the white bread, white shape in the pumpernickel.

● Shape toast is a fun food. Just use a cookie cutter to make shapes from bread. Prepare as you would French toast. Refrigerate extras in a plastic bag and kids can heat them up in the microwave. They can be eaten with syrup or used to make a hot ham and cheese sandwich.

Use bags, glass or plastic containers, but be sure they're especially designed for freezing.

FREEZER FACTS

*M*ost people don't have the time to can or preserve foods anymore. But freezing is so quick and easy, almost anyone can save time and money by learning how to freeze fresh foods. Here are a few *Better Living* tips.

● Freeze produce as soon as you bring it home. Every minute between picking and packing means lost quality.

● Wash everything thoroughly. Not only will it remove dirt, but it will help remove any pesticides on the skin.

● Make sure your freezer temperature is at zero or below. You can buy an inexpensive thermometer to keep in the freezer.

● It's important to blanch or scald most vegetables. It helps to stop natural enzymes that can cause spoilage. Just place vegetables in a metal colander and submerge them in boiling water for 1 to 3 minutes.

● Work with small batches. Trim, blanch, and freeze a few containers, then go back and repeat the process.

● Mark each container with contents and date.

● Remember that it's a lot easier to mark freezer bags before filling.

Fruits can be frozen dry or in liquid, but those packed in syrup will be firmer and juicier when thawed.

● Remove as much air as possible from freezer bags. Use a soda straw to syphon out the last bit of air and cause the bag to collapse against the contents.

● To make a light syrup, boil 2 parts of water with 1 part sugar. Chill; then pour about 1/2 cup over each 2 cups of fruit.

FRUIT

*N*o matter how you slice it, fresh fruit is a great nutritional bargain. But here are a few things that may help you get a little more for your money.

● Wash everything before eating, even if you plan to peel it. Contamination and pesticides on the skin can be transferred to the fruit during preparation.

● Fruits ripen in different ways. Some ripen best on the vine, while others taste better if they're picked green and then allowed to mature.

● Fruits that will continue to ripen after they've been picked are avocados, bananas, and honeydews. Try to buy these fruits a little green and plan to eat them when they ripen.

● Apricots, nectarines, peaches, pears, and plums will continue to ripen off the vine if they are stored in a closed container such as a brown paper bag. Once they've become ripe, place them in a plastic bag in the refrigerator.

● Apples, berries, grapes, grapefruit, and pineapples will only ripen on the plant, so you must buy them fully ripe and ready to eat.

● Avocados will not continue to ripen once they've been cut open.

● When selecting grapes, pick up a bunch and shake it gently. Grapes that cling to the stem are most likely fresh and sweet. If they fall off, they're probably old and tart tasting.

● Grapes with a brown or grayish color are most likely to be sour.

● Grapes will last 5 to 7 days if refrigerated.

Green bananas ripen more quickly when placed near a ripe banana.

● Bananas ripen best off the tree. It's a good idea to buy them green, in various stages of ripeness so that they can ripen as you need them, not all at one time.

● Refrigerating bananas may cause the skin to darken but will not affect the fruit inside.

● Be sure to separate bananas from the top knot with a knife when you bring them home. Pulling bananas from a dried stem can create tiny splits in the skins, which can cause the fruit to spoil quickly.

● Leave unripe bananas at room temperature until ready to use.

● The best raspberries are a deep magenta color and dry to the touch. Lighter pink berries are underripe and sour.

● Wet and sticky berries are probably old and musty tasting. Look in the bottom of the package for juice. If it's wet, don't buy them.

● Fresh cranberries should bounce when dropped. Select berries that are very hard and brightly colored.

● Only cook cranberries until they "pop." Cooking longer will cause them to become bitter.

● Refrigerate apples, apricots, berries, grapes, cherries, peaches, pears, and plums. All other fruits can be kept at room temperature or a little cooler.

● To select the best grapefruit, pick out a few that look firm and glossy, then weigh them on the produce scale. The heaviest ones will be the juiciest.

● Don't buy a grapefruit that feels spongy. The best ones will be firm and have a pleasant citrus smell.

● As a rule, Florida grapefruits tend to be juicier than those grown in western states.

● Grapefruit grown in western states tends to have a thicker skin and be easier to peel.

A little salt can make a grapefruit taste sweeter.

● White grapefruit has a stronger flavor than pink grapefruit.

● To select a ripe cantaloupe, smell the stem end. A good one will smell ripe and sweet. If it's underripe, there will be little smell.

● Don't buy a cantaloupe if the stem is still attached or the scar is rough and misshappen; the fruit may not ripen well.

● Choose a cantaloupe with a depressed scar on the stem end.

● Look for an even yellow color to the netting design on the cantaloupe skin and little or no green.

● An overripe cantaloupe will have a thick, sweet odor with a hint of spoilage.

● Watermelons should be smooth and green with a waxy look to the rind. The resting side (the side that lies against the ground) will be yellow.

● "Thump" a watermelon and listen for an indication of ripeness. A high, thin sound means it's not yet ripe; a deep, low tone suggests the melon is ready to eat.

● Don't toss leftover watermelon. Puree it in a food processor, remove the seeds, and freeze it into juice pops.

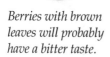 

Berries with brown leaves will probably have a bitter taste.

S T R A W B E R R I E S

*I*t's a sign of the season: devoted strawberry lovers, down on their knees, working their way through rows of fruit. Picking your own strawberries may seem like a lot of work, but the taste of berries, bright red and still warm from the field, is well worth the effort. Whether you pick your own or pick them out at the grocery store, here's what you need to know.

● In the store, the best-tasting berries will be bright red and plump with an intense strawberry aroma. Berries with pink skin and no scent are underripe and will taste sour.

● Once picked, berries will not continue to ripen.

● Tiny, misshapen berries are usually hard and flavorless.

● A leaking package is a bad sign. Some of the berries are probably damaged and will quickly contaminate the entire container.

● Be very gentle when handling berries; rough handling will cause them to spoil faster than anything else.

● Pick berries by pinching the stem. Pulling on the fruit can bruise it.

● Don't pull off the green cap. Once the cap is removed, the berry will begin to lose moisture and deteriorate.

● Look for medium to small size berries because they tend to be sweeter and more flavorful.

● Extremely large berries will likely be hollow in the middle and not have much taste.

● Don't put all your berries in one basket. Too much weight will crush the berries on the bottom. It's better to use several small containers.

● Berries will only stay fresh for one or two days, so only pick what you can eat or preserve in that amount of time.

● Never put berries in the trunk of your car. The heat can cause them to spoil more quickly. Instead, put a cooler in your car so that you can chill your berries immediately. Once you get home, spread the berries out on a cookie sheet and remove any damaged ones to prevent them from spoiling the whole batch.

Pick only perfect berries. One bad fruit will cause the others to begin to spoil even before you get them home.

● Washing strawberries will cause them to deteriorate more quickly. Store them unwashed in the refrigerator in a colander or berry basket. This will allow the cold air to circulate through the fruit more effectively.

● Professional chefs prefer to store berries on a cookie sheet lined with a paper towel. Do not allow berries to touch.

● In Venice, strawberries are served with a wedge of lemon and sugar.

● The French serve strawberries topped with a splash of red wine vinegar.

● In England, fresh strawberries served with cream are considered an elegant dessert.

Food

The larger the hole in a navel orange, the more likely it is to be sweet.

CITRUS FRUIT

The tangy taste of citrus is abundant during the winter months. Like anything else, there's a lot we can learn to help squeeze the most out of oranges, lemons, and limes.

● When selecting citrus fruits for juice, judge by weight rather than by size. The heavier the fruit, the juicier it's likely to be.

● For orange juice, the Valencia orange is generally considered the best.

● Navel oranges or Florida Temple oranges are considered the best for eating.

● Don't judge the quality of an orange by color, because they're often dyed to improve their appearance. Brown spots on the skin can actually indicate good quality.

● A green orange is not usually underripe. The color comes from a natural process called "regreening." These oranges can be sweet and delicious.

● Don't spend extra money for fancy Mandarin oranges. Mandarin oranges are the same as tangerines. The only difference is where they're grown.

● When selecting lemons, look for a smooth skin and small points on each end. They tend to be juicier and more flavorful.

● Get the most juice from a lemon by heating it slightly in warm water and rolling it on the counter to soften it up.

● It takes about six lemons to yield one cup of juice.

● To use just a small amount of lemon juice for tea or flavoring, pierce the lemon with a toothpick and squeeze out the desired amount. Then replace the toothpick in the hole to keep the lemon fresh.

To make cake frosting extra white, add a little squirt of lemon juice.

● A teaspoon of lemon juice will act as a dough conditioner for bread in a bread machine. It will help increase the volume of the loaf.

● Soak a whole lemon in hot water for a few minutes to get nearly double the amount of juice.

● Use a nutcracker to squeeze juice from a lemon half.

● You can freeze whole lemons in a large zip-lock bag. Just dip them in water and pop them in the bag. Then when you need fresh lemon juice, thaw in the microwave, let sit for a few minutes, then squeeze out the juice.

● Soak unpeeled oranges in boiling water for a few minutes. When you peel the orange, the entire white membrane will slip off with the peel and leave you a perfect orange.

● Never discard citrus rinds. Grate and freeze them to use for flavoring fish, poultry, and desserts.

● When selecting a pineapple, look for one that is large and heavy. Dark green leaves are also a sign of freshness.

● Keep a pineapple fresher by slicing from the bottom as you use it, leaving the green top intact.

● A pineapple will not continue to ripen once it is picked. If you find a pineapple is underripe, cut off the top and remove the skin. Slice the fruit and boil for 5 minutes in a little sugar water. After it cools, it will taste freshly picked.

● Make fresh pineapple juice the way processing plants do. Grind all the pineapple trimmings in a blender or food processor, strain, and drink.

Boil lemon rinds and use the liquid to make tangy iced tea. It's also great mixed with fruit juice.

● To counteract cooking odors, place an unpeeled lemon in the oven at 300 degrees for about 15 minutes. Turn off the oven and open the door a bit. The kitchen will smell fresh and clean.

● Because of their acidic content, lemons make an excellent marinade for seafood and poultry. For a simple one, just blend olive oil, herbs, and lemon juice.

● Once the juice is gone, lemons are still useful. Sprinkle with coarse salt and rub on copper pans for a bright shine. It really works.

● Use a hollowed-out lemon half as a holder when working with steel wool.

● Grind used lemons, followed by hot water, in the garbage disposal to keep it smelling fresh.

● Prevent lemons, oranges, and limes from shrinking and wilting by storing them in a container of water kept in the refrigerator. You may need a small saucer or some other object to weight them down.

HAVE YOUR CAKE

When baking a cake from scratch, all ingredients should be at room temperature.

A homemade cake is the center of attention on the table, and for birthday celebrations it is often the only food we serve. Cake mixes are convenient, but there's a real creative pleasure to learning to bake one or two special cakes from scratch. Experienced bakers have many secrets to ensure success. Here are a few of the best.

● For a moister cake, add 2 tablespoons of oil to a cake mix, then follow directions.

● To prevent a cake from becoming too brown and drying out, place a pan of water on the top rack of the oven while baking.

● Another way to ensure a moist cake is to place it in the refrigerator immediately after baking.

● Don't overbeat a cake batter. It can cause the cake to crack.

● Spray the beaters of your electric mixer with cooking spray to keep batter from clinging.

● Be sure to carefully flour sides of cake pan. Spots left uncovered by flour will prevent cake from gripping the sides while rising, and force it to slide back down.

● For the same reason, do not use butter to grease a cake pan. Flour cannot cling to it evenly.

● Chocolate cakes are notorious for sticking. Be extra careful when you grease and flour the pan.

Instead of flour, you can dust the pan with cocoa or even a little cake mix.

● As an extra precaution, fit a piece of wax or parchment paper into the bottom of the cake pan when you're baking a chocolate cake.

A frozen cake is much easier to frost than a fresh one.

● To fit paper exactly, trace the bottom of your cake pan on to the paper and trim to size.

● It's much easier to dust pans if you keep a supply of flour in a large shaker.

● Instead of greasing and flouring pans, you can use a product called Baker's Joy®, which is recommended by many professional bakers. Since it just sprays into the pan, it's a lot neater and faster. It's available in many grocery stores.

● In a pinch, create your own cake flour by blending 2 tablespoons of cornstarch with 1 cup of all-purpose flour.

● Cakes should be baked in the center of the oven.

● If a cake rises too much in the center, you can push it back down by placing a smaller pan on top of the cake and gently applying pressure to the cake.

● To prevent a cake from sticking to the platter, sprinkle it first with sugar. The slices will lift off easily.

● Freeze a cake first before cutting into decorative shapes.

● To prevent cake crumbs from marring the frosting, many bakers apply a crumb glaze. That's a very thin layer of frosting that coats the cake and seals in any crumbs. Allow it to dry, then frost as usual.

● To be sure you get the right shade, blend colored frostings in advance and allow them to sit. Food coloring intensifies over time.

Angel food and other sponge-type cakes must always cool upside down to prevent them from collapsing.

● Bevel the frosting around the edges of a cake to prevent it from cracking.

● To get perfect results when writing on a cake, first write on the frosting with a toothpick; then trace over the marks with decorator frosting.

● When slicing, always slide the knife out, never bring it back up through the cake.

● Make a heart-shaped cake without using special pans. Bake a cake using one round and one square pan. Cut the round layer in half. Place the square layer on a large platter with one corner to the top, diamond shape. Lay the round layers on either side.

To help keep cake fresh, store half an apple in the same container.

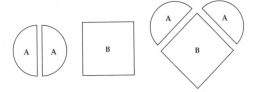

● Create a butterfly cake with round cake pans. Slice round layers in half and place the rounded ends together with the sliced sides facing out to make butterfly wings. Frost with various colors.

● Top a cake with colored coconut. Just put shredded coconut in a zip-lock bag. Add a little liquid food coloring and shake.

● To decorate a cake without frosting, lay a leaf, paper heart, or some other flat shape in the middle of the cake and sprinkle around it with powdered sugar. Remove the shape and the design will be on the cake.

● Don't apply powdered sugar too soon before serving, because the sugar can be absorbed by the cake.

● If you heat a knife in hot water and wipe it dry before slicing a cake, the frosting won't stick to the knife.

● Slice creamy cakes, like cheese cake, with a long piece of unwaxed dental floss. Hold it taut and pull it down through the cake. This will also work for a hot cake.

Use a drip style coffee maker. Nearly all experts agree that the drip method produces the very best coffee.

COFFEE

Coffee is expensive, and most of us don't know beans about it. Because it's estimated that the average American will consume nearly 60,000 cups in a lifetime, it's a good idea to learn how to make the most of it. Here are a few tips.

- Coffee beans determine the quality of coffee.

- Arabica beans produce a very high-quality drink.

- Robusta beans are more common, but they lack the quality and flavor of Arabica beans.

- Robusta beans tend to be higher in caffeine.

- The finer the grind, the stronger the brew. Finely ground coffee will produce a stronger drink than will the same amount of more coarsely ground coffee.

- Home-style drip coffee makers do not raise the water temperature as hot as a commercial machine. That's why the flavor at home tends to be less intense than in a real coffee house.

- The better the water, the better your coffee will be. If your tap water has a slightly off taste, it will affect the flavor of your coffee.

- Try brewing your coffee with distilled water. Not only will it taste better, but there are no minerals to clog up your coffee maker.

- Make sure your coffee maker is clean. Residue from oils can significantly alter the taste of coffee.

- Clean your machine by running a full pot of white vinegar through the brewing cycle, followed by another cycle using fresh water.

• Never allow coffee to sit on a hot plate. Direct heat can cause a chemical breakdown of coffee oils and ruin the flavor. Instead, transfer freshly brewed coffee to a thermal container.

Use frozen coffee cubes to cool hot cups of coffee without diluting the flavor.

• Freshly ground beans make the best coffee. Coffee begins to lose its flavor the minute the beans are ground.

• If you prefer to buy it already ground, brick-pack packaging tends to keep it fresher. If you like to buy it on sale, this is the best type for stocking up. An unopened brick pack can be kept on the shelf for about a year.

• Purists say that ground coffee will stay fresh for only a week or two in the refrigerator. Those with less discerning tastes say it can last two months without serious loss of quality.

• Use leftover coffee to make frozen cubes. They're great in iced coffee, but can also be used in chocolate drinks for a mocha flavor.

• Make your own flavored coffees by adding a little fresh cinnamon, vanilla, or even a dash of peppermint to the grounds before brewing.

• When serving coffee later in the day, make a 50/50 blend of decaf and regular coffee to create your own light brew. This is usually a good compromise when you're serving several people.

• Most experts believe that the "Swiss Water" method used to decaffeinate coffee is superior to other methods. Look for it on the coffee label.

• You can make individual servings of cafe au lait by boiling a half cup of milk in the microwave and adding hot coffee to the cup.

• If you use paper coffee filters, you can separate them more easily by turning the whole stack inside out. Then, they'll easily separate one-by-one.

Smaller apples will stay fresher longer than large ones, so only buy large ones when you plan to eat them right away.

APPLES

*A*mericans love apples. Actually, they are our most popular fruit. And we probably have Johnny Appleseed to thank for their abundance. His goal was to plant seedlings all across the country, but sad to say, he only made it to Ft. Wayne, IN. No matter though; it was a great start. Here are some tips to help you enjoy an all-American favorite.

● Always store apples in the refrigerator. Apples kept at room temperature will spoil 8 to 10 times faster than those kept cool.

● Most apples will keep 3 to 5 weeks in the refrigerator.

● Apples can be stored for a longer period of time if they don't touch one another.

● Apples should be wiped dry before being stored for a long period of time.

● Some varieties of apples will taste different based on the time of year you buy them.

● Store apples in a ventilated plastic bag or refrigerator drawer. Avoid storing them with other fruits and vegetables because they can affect the flavor of other foods.

● Freeze extra apples when they're in season and flavor is at its peak. It's best to sprinkle them with lemon juice or ascorbic acid to prevent browning.

● To prevent wasting fruit, use a vegetable peeler instead of a knife when removing skins.

● Core apples more easily by first slicing off a small piece from the top and bottom, so that you can clearly see the center of the apple.

- To help baked apples hold their shape, use a peeler to remove a thin strip of skin from around the center. Then bake them in a muffin tin.

- Apples come in hundreds of varieties. Basically, tart apples are best for cooking, and sweeter apples are best eaten raw.

- Here's a quick idea for individual apple tarts. It's a simple guaranteed hit!

Cut ready-made pie crust into an apple shape (small enough to hold in your hand). Fill with sliced apples, sprinkle with cinnamon and sugar. Top with a second crust, crimp around the edges with a fork. Add a little pastry stem and leaf on top, then bake.

Only slice apples with a stainless steel knife. Carbon will discolor the flesh.

Dough can be shaped and kept frozen for up to a month.

BREADMAKERS

*D*on't think of automatic breadmakers as just another luxury appliance. Even the most basic model can turn out fresh, preservative-free bread for just pennies a loaf. The machine does most of the work, so even the busiest cook can find the time to create delicious breads and rolls. It couldn't be easier. Anyway you slice it, it's a great way to save a little dough. Here are some tips to get the most out of your machine.

● Always use bread flour. It contains a higher gluten content and will produce a higher, more attractive loaf.

● Use regular whole-wheat flour instead of ground whole-wheat flour. Ground whole-wheat flour has a coarse texture that won't allow the dough to rise well.

● Buy yeast in bulk at a warehouse store. You can save a small fortune over those little packets.

● It's OK to peek inside during the kneading process. Actually, it will allow you to become familiar with the proper dough consistency.

● Weather can affect the flour's ability to absorb moisture. So, on humid days add a little more flour; on very dry days, a little less.

● Dough can be stored well-covered in the refrigerator, for 1 or 2 days before baking. Store in a well-oiled bowl.

● Experiment with brands of yeast. There is a difference.

- Never store baked bread in the refrigerator because it will go stale much faster. It should stay fresh for 2 or 3 days.

- For a softer crust, seal the bread in a plastic bag while it's still warm.

- For a crisper crust, allow more air circulation by storing it in a lightly closed paper bag.

- To help activate yeast, place the sugar right next to the yeast in the bottom of the bread baking pan.

- Rye flour tends to yield a small loaf. To strengthen the structure of the loaf, replace 1/4 cup liquid with an egg to give the bread better volume. You can do this even if egg is not called for in the recipe.

- Sometimes bread won't rise because there is not enough sugar in the recipe. The general rule of thumb is 1 tablespoon of sugar for every cup of flour.

- Too much sugar will also prevent bread from rising well. This usually happens when the recipe calls for fruit. In this case, decrease the sugar a bit.

- Add a teaspoon of lemon juice to condition the dough and help to increase the volume of the loaf.

- Be sure to wash and rinse the bread pan and mixing blade thoroughly. Soap residue can affect the quality of your next baking project.

- Spray a small amount of cooking spray on the mixing blade. It will help remove the blade from the dough.

- To make specialty dinner rolls, simply let the machine prepare the dough, then turn it out on a floured surface.

- Make clover leaf rolls by shaping the dough into small balls and snipping an "X" shape on the top with well-floured scissors.

Try to avoid using well water; it can affect the baking process.

Remember that shiny pans make a light crust, dark pans make a darker crust.

● Cutting with a knife will flatten the dough. Instead use a piece of dental floss. Shape the dough into a log. Slip the dental floss underneath, then pull the ends up and cross them until they cut through the dough. Repeat.

● To save time, pre-mix dry ingredients for several batches of bread and store in zip-lock bags. Then just dump the contents and add liquid ingredients.

Quick Guide
to Measurements

onverting measurements can be tricky. Here's a quick list of the measurements you'll most likely need to convert in the kitchen.

1 tablespoon = 3 teaspoons

1/4 cup = 4 tablespoons

1/2 cup = 8 tablespoons

1 cup = 16 tablespoons

1 pint = 2 cups

1 quart = 4 cups

1 gallon = 4 quarts

1 gallon = 16 cups

1 fluid ounce = 2 tablespoons

1 jigger = 1 1/2 ounces

1 cup = 8 ounces

1 pint = 16 ounces

1 quart = 32 ounces

1 pound = 16 ounces

EQUIVALENTS

*S*ometimes it's handy to know the equivalents of common foods. It makes planning recipes a lot easier when you can mentally measure in advance. It can also make shopping simpler when you know the equivalent amounts of a fresh or canned ingredient. Because fresh foods vary in size, equivalents are approximate, but they'll give you a good idea of how much you'll need. Here are some of the most common.

1 pound cottage cheese = 2 cups

8 ounces cream cheese = 1 cup or 16 tablespoons

1/4 pound hard cheese = 1 cup shredded

1 stick butter = 1/2 cup or 8 tablespoons

1 cup heavy cream = 2 cups whipped

1 pound loaf bread = 12 to 16 slices

1 cup bread crumbs = 3 to 4 slices dry bread

1 cup uncooked macaroni =2 cups cooked

1 pound coffee = 80 tablespoons or 40 cups

1 pound tea = 125 cups

1 large egg = 1/4 cup

1 medium egg = 1/5 cup

1 small egg = 1/6 cup

1 pound flour = 4 cups sifted

3 teaspoons baking powder = 1 ounce

1 square baking chocolate = 1 ounce

1 pound granulated sugar = 2 cups

1 pound brown sugar = 2 1/4 cups

1 pound confectioners sugar = 4 cups

1/8 teaspoon artificial sweetener = 1 teaspoon sugar

1 clove garlic = 1/8 teaspoon

1 medium onion = 1/2 cup chopped

1 teaspoon dried herbs = 1 tablespoon fresh

1 pound fresh tomatoes = 1 1/3 cups

1 pound fresh mushrooms = 6 ounces canned

1 quart berries = 3 1/2 cups

1 lemon = 2 to 3 tablespoons juice

1 cup pecans = 4 1/4 ounces chopped

1 pound raw potatoes = 2 cups mashed

1 pound raw potatoes = 3 - 4 medium sized potatoes

Kids

Every year the statisticians release the estimated cost of raising a child. And every year parents are staggered by the prospect. But kids are not statistics, and the cost of raising them is a blend of time, money, and attention, all of which are in limited supply. In this section, we've collected lots of ideas to help stretch the time and money available for the most important job in the world.

BUDGET BABIES

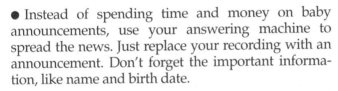here's a real baby boomlet going on out there, and with each new baby comes a surprised set of parents who wonder how someone so small can be so expensive. Here are a few *Better Living* tips to save a little of the time and money it takes to bring up baby.

Never buy a used car seat. Many older models don't meet safety standards, and some could be damaged in ways that are not obvious.

● Instead of spending time and money on baby announcements, use your answering machine to spread the news. Just replace your recording with an announcement. Don't forget the important information, like name and birth date.

● Breast feeding is considered to be the best method of feeding baby, but millions of infants thrive on the bottle. If you choose to bottle feed, remember that powdered formulas are significantly cheaper than ready mixed.

● Make your own baby food. Just puree fresh foods and freeze in ice cube containers. Soft foods like bananas and cooked potatoes can simply be mashed with a fork, but others can be quickly prepared in a food processor or hand-held grinder.

● Bathe baby in the sink instead of a special tub. Wear soft cotton gloves to keep baby from slipping and to serve as a convenient wash cloth. It's a lot easier to clean those little ears and toes, too.

● Frozen french fries make wonderful teethers. They're easy to hold, and just the right size to fit into little mouths to soothe sore gums.

● Frozen vegetables make a great snack for tots. They love the icy sweetness and will often eat vegetables that they would never touch on a dinner plate.

Instead of a changing table use a dresser or dry sink covered with a waterproof pad.

● Check out your health department for free immunizations. Many offer everything baby needs for free.

● Don't spend money on shoes for infants. Most pediatricians agree that babies really need bare feet to get a good feel for the floor while they're learning to balance and walk. Little socks to keep their feet warm is all they need.

● Check out thrift stores and classified ads for used baby equipment. With smaller families these days, lots of high quality baby equipment is discarded long before it's worn out.

● Check with your insurance company for special prices on car seats. Some companies offer seats at a reduced price to their clients.

● A dimmer switch on an overhead light in a baby's room will make it easier to peek in at night. It can also work as a night light when a young child is afraid of the dark.

● Make your own baby wipes. Here's how.

BUDGET BABY WIPES

1 roll Bounty® or microwave quality paper towels.
(Use small-size towels or cut a small roll in half
with a serrated knife.)
2 1/4 cups water
2 tablespoons baby shampoo
1 tablespoon baby oil

Remove the cardboard container from the center of towels.
Mix liquid ingredients in a plastic container.
Place roll in container and turn upside-down and soak overnight.
When ready to use, pull towel from the center of the roll.
Because these wipes have no preservatives, they should be kept in an airtight container and used within a week or so.

● Organize baby pictures by year. Just toss pictures in shoe boxes marked age 1, 2, 3, etc. When you have time, you can put the best ones in the baby book.

Don't buy a walker. They can be very dangerous and experts say they can actually impede a child from learning to walk.

● Create a yearbook. Use a three-ring binder and enclose the best of your child's art work, report cards, awards, and even pictures for each school year. This is a wonderful way to keep things neat and orderly without a lot of effort.

● Keep a portable tape recorder handy to record important moments in the first few years of baby's life. Most parents are too busy to write things down, and nobody ever remembers the date that little Kate took her first steps. Be sure to record those cute first words, too. It will be a treasure later on.

● If you don't have time to keep a diary, jot down baby's milestones or cute words on your daily calendar. You'll have a record of important dates and special memories. Later you can put them in a baby book.

CUTTING KIDS' HAIR

*E*ven the prettiest babies can benefit from a little expert hair care. But before you tote the little ones off to the beauty shop for a trim, consider saving time and money by doing it yourself. Here's what you need to know.

● All children's hair needs to be trimmed regularly. Even little baldies can benefit from a few snips. Hair experts say that regular trimming up until about age 2 can actually help determine growth patterns in hair.

● Older kids should sit on a phone book or on something high enough to bring them to eye level with the scissors.

● Use a smock or towel to keep prickly hairs off of little necks.

● Forget the sewing scissors or kitchen shears. Invest in good, sharp hair cutting scissors about 5 inches long. The right tools always make the job easier, and they can pay for themselves in one good haircut.

● Lightly spray hair with warm water. Damp hair is easier to control and will help you to cut straighter.

● Keep talking. Most really bad mistakes are made because kids get restless and wiggle. Keeping their attention prevents them from getting bored and fidgety.

● Cut bangs from the outside of one eyebrow to the other, no wider than temple to temple.

● Remember that curls bounce up, so be sure to cut curly hair about a half-inch longer than you want it to look when you're finished.

- Because children's hair is so delicate, it needs special treatment. Only use gentle shampoos designed for kids.

Cut from right to left if you're right-handed, and the opposite way if you're left-handed.

- Never use a lemon rinse or conditioner on a child's hair.

- Treat cradle cap, the scaly condition on a baby's scalp, by gently rubbing a little olive oil into the scalp, and very lightly massaging with a soft brush to remove the scales. Always be extremely gentle with an infant.

- Even though lots of kids love curls, most experts don't recommend a perm for anyone under age 10. The chemicals are too harsh.

Knowing what you need to do is the first step toward getting it done.

HOMEWORK HELPERS

*H*omework hassles are commonplace in busy households. But most teachers agree that a student who has a handle on homework is more likely to succeed academically. Here are some tips to help develop a good family homework plan.

● Help kids understand that homework is not optional. Even if there are no specific assignments, the best students have a habit of studying every night.

● Make sure students have a special notebook to record assignments.

● Have kids post homework assignments on the fridge or some other common area. When parents know assignment deadlines, they can do a better job of helping kids stay on schedule.

● Make a schedule to help organize activities. Use a chart and include things like sports, piano lessons, and, of course, homework. Don't allow extra-curricular activities to steal away regular study time.

● Designate a study site and always have kids do homework there. Working in the same quiet place will help develop good work habits.

● Make sure that kids have plenty of materials such as pencils, dictionary and other reference books.

● Make homework time a family activity. While kids study, adults can use the time to do paper work such as paying bills or reading the paper. It eliminates distractions and teaches kids to concentrate on the task at hand.

● Have kids reread chapters from the beginning that they can read quickly, and slow down when they come across something that they don't remember.

● Help kids develop a long- and short-term study plan. Short-term tasks include homework that needs to be completed tonight; a long-term plan is for term papers and tests.

Keep work organized. Make a filing system out of a cardboard box to store homework and other papers.

● Insist that kids review work they already know. Experts say this is a key to good memory and strong skills. As with athletes, the best performances come from lots of practice.

● When reviewing, concentrate on the most difficult material.

● The more often kids review, the more they learn. It's better to review something three times for 20 minutes than only once for an hour.

● Save tests and quizzes and use them when studying for year-end exams. Quizzes usually contain only the most important material kids need to know.

● Consider a study group. Sometimes kids are more willing to study when they can invite a friend or two over to help. Experts say that study groups can be very helpful.

● Post important words or terms around the house, such as on the bathroom mirror or the closet door. Then the whole family can help by asking questions.

Consider matching your child's savings. A dollar-for-dollar match is a real incentive to save.

KIDS AND MONEY

American kids have a lot of pocket money. In the early '90s a study showed that kids ages 4 to 12 spent over $7 billion. That's why it's never too soon to teach your kids the value of a dollar. Here are some tips from the experts.

● Give children an allowance. At around 5 or 6, begin giving them about $1 a week. Then increase it each year by $1.

● Give consistently. The amount is less important than learning to deal with money on a schedule.

● Don't tie money to grades or regular chores. An allowance should only be a means of learning how to handle money.

● Encourage kids to save. A see-through bank or glass jar can be an excellent tool to help young children see how money accumulates.

● Don't use a piggy bank that is too large. Filling an over-sized container can simply be too overwhelming for a young child. They'll get frustrated before they can see results.

● Teach kids about both long-term and short-term saving. Insist that they save some money in a college fund, which is long-term, and the rest in a short-term fund, which can be used for toys and other fun things.

● Help kids buy stock. Owning a single share of their favorite video game or fast food company can help them understand how the economy works.

● Set up a home checking account. Let older children use an old checkbook to withdraw money from an allowance account. This can help them learn money management.

• Encourage kids to start a small business. Cutting grass, baking cookies, or helping neighborhood moms can help pre-teens earn extra money and, most important, teach them the value of work.

*Introduce kids to **Zillions**, a consumer report magazine for pre-teens featuring articles about money from a kid's point of view.*

• Never allow a child to skip a family chore because he or she has found a way to earn money. Children need to learn how to balance both work and household responsibilities.

• Without financial advice, children and their money will soon be parted. So it's important to let children make small money mistakes now instead of big money mistakes later.

A bag of dried beans can be fun for a child learning to pour and fill containers. They can be scooped up and stored in a container and reused.

HOMEMADE PLAYTHINGS

Keeping kids supplied with creative playthings can be expensive. But many of the old favorites can be made at home for less money, and more fun than the commercial variety. Even wealthy parents know that it's unwise to give children the impression that everything needs to be bought in a toy store. Here are some ideas for things you can do yourself without a lot of time or money.

● Create huge and fantastic bubbles by mixing up your own bubble recipe. In a half gallon jug, mix 1 cup dishwashing liquid (Dawn® works particularly well), and fill the rest with water. Outdoors, pour about 2 inches in a cake pan and have fun.

● Experiment with creative bubble wands. Some great ones are strawberry baskets, which make amazing bubble clusters; plastic holders for soft drink six-packs; and even old frames (minus the lenses) from sunglasses.

● Make finger paints with a can of inexpensive shaving cream and a few drops of food coloring. Squirt the cream on a cookie sheet and let kids blend the color with their fingers. This is also great in the tub. Let kids "paint" the walls (it's best not to overdo it with the food coloring).

● Small magnets are a lot of fun for little kids. Tie one to the end of a homemade fishing pole. Scatter paper clips for fish and let the kids have fun. Magnet tape is a great product that is sticky on one side and magnetized on the other. Just cut a piece and stick it to the back of pictures, letters, or anything you want to hang on the fridge or other metal object.

● A magnifying glass can be a real adventure for younger children. They can spend hours wandering the yard looking for bugs, flowers, or anything that catches their fancy.

● Pipe cleaners are great for almost anything. They can easily be twisted into rings, crowns, antlers, candy canes, eyeglasses, and anything else their imagination can come up with. They're great to keep in the car for those times when tots need a little diversion.

A large bag of multi-colored pompons is another great toy. Kids love to throw them, glue them, "cook" with them, dump them, and sort them by color.

● Stringing colorful macaroni helps develop small motor skills and costs a lot less than bead kits. In a zip-lock plastic bag, combine 2 tablespoons rubbing alcohol, a few drops of food coloring, and a handful of macaroni (select a shape that's easy to string). Work it around in the bag until pasta is dyed. Dump contents onto newspaper and allow to dry. To make stringing easier, wrap one end of a string with a scotch tape to keep it stiff.

● Make a piñata by filling an old paper grocery bag with candy and trinkets. Let kids help decorate it with crayons, paper, and glue. Then tie the top closed with heavy string and yarn. Hang outdoors and let kids try to break it open with a stick. This is great entertainment for parties.

● Make your own playing dough by cooking up this simple recipe. A little food coloring allows you to create interesting shades you can't buy in the store, and this recipe develops a really pleasant consistency.

PLAYING DOUGH

Mix in a medium pot:
   1 cup flour
   1/2 cup salt
   2 tablespoons cream of tartar
Add:
   1 cup water
   2 teaspoons vegetable food coloring

Let kids create an edible Noah's Ark with canned frosting and store-bought animal cookies.

Cook over medium heat and stir about 3 to 5 minutes. It will look like a globby mess, but keep stirring. Once the mixture thickens into a doughy consistency, remove from heat. Let it cool for several minutes and knead slightly to make sure that ingredients are thoroughly blended. Store in an airtight container or plastic bag. And just like the real stuff, it's best used on a washable surface.

KITCHEN KALEIDOSCOPE

In a shallow glass baking dish, pour about an inch and a half of whole milk. Then squirt in food coloring; use several drops of each color but do not allow colors to touch. Use red in one area, blue in another, etc. Then add a few drops of dishwashing detergent. The colors will all begin to swirl around, making beautiful patterns, just like a kaleidoscope. When movement slows down, just add a few more drops of detergent. Actually, it's a science lesson: the detergent is causing the fat in the milk to separate.

HOMEMADE ICE CREAM

Kids can make their own homemade ice cream. Instead of an ice cream maker, all you need are two coffee cans, one large, one small.

In a clean 1 pound coffee can, mix:
1 cup whipping cream
1/2 teaspoon vanilla
1/2 cup sugar
1 cup whole milk
chopped fresh fruit or berries
food coloring if desired
Seal the can with the plastic lid.

Place the small can inside the larger one and pack ice into the large can to completely surround the small one. Sprinkle 1 cup of rock salt on top, and close the large can with the plastic lid.

Let kids roll the can around on the floor for 10 minutes or so.

Open both cans, scrape the ice cream from the sides and close. Repack with fresh ice and salt and close securely. Let the kids roll the can for few more minutes until the ice cream is hard. Kids love to peek inside to check!

When you have several children, it's fun to make a few batches at once and create several different flavors.

KIDS AND READING

Read aloud to older children. Even 10- and 12-year-olds can be captivated by a good story. It also presents a good opportunity for conversation.

Children's books are big business and kids' favorites can easily cost from $2 to $20. To help develop their children's reading skills, some well-meaning parents spend a small fortune on the latest books. But the experts say it's just not necessary. Here's their advice.

● Take children to the library. Free story hours are a wonderful introduction to the world of books and reading.

● Borrow lots of books on a regular basis. Let children help decide which ones to take home. Then, after reading, decide which ones you might buy.

● Read aloud to your child. Even small babies love the rhythm and sound of language.

● Have older kids read to little ones. This develops skills for both of them.

● Record stories on a tape recorder. That way, kids can hear you read their favorites even when you're not there. Let them follow along with the book.

● Be sure books are age appropriate. Little children need lots of pictures and just a few words. The text shouldn't be overwhelming.

Make sure children see you read. They love to imitate adult behavior.

● Kids of all ages love videos. Borrow the book and video version of the same story and help your child compare the differences.

● Borrow a book for yourself. The *New York Times Parent's Guide to the Best Books for Children* is a great way to learn about reading for kids.

CUTTING THE HIGH COST OF KIDS

Shop the discount stores. Most children under 8 couldn't care less where you shop for their things.

*S*ince the experts say that a child born in the '90s will cost well over $200,000 to raise to age 18, it's a good idea to try to cut the high cost of kid stuff. There are lots of things you can do, and with some practice there might even be a little left over to spend on yourself.

● Get the kids involved in the shopping process. Even at age 5 or 6, children can begin to learn about value. It's amazing how thrifty a 12-year-old can be when he or she has learned to compare prices and quality.

● Put some effort into extending the life of kids' clothes. The real expense comes when you have to constantly replace outfits because they've been ruined by stains or tears.

● Try to buy play clothes in mostly dark colors and prints. It's a fact of life that kids stain everything they wear, so try to buy things that keep stains from showing up.

● Protect white collars, sneakers, and other light-colored things with a spray fabric protector before kids even put them on.

● Teach kids how to use a stain stick and keep a couple handy at home and in the car. When spills occur, just rub with the stick to prevent the stain from setting (stain sticks are available at the grocery store).

● Don't supply kids with guaranteed stain makers. If it's all the same to your kids, buy light-colored juice, ice pops, and other messy snacks. Avoid any paints, chalks, and markers that aren't clearly washable.

Shop in advance. Buy holiday and party clothes early. Waiting until the last minute usually means you'll end up spending more than you need to.

● Make sure that each child has an outfit to be worn only for church or special occasions. Teach them to keep it clean and to change the minute they get home. It's good discipline, and you'll never have to run out and pay full price when a special occasion comes up.

● Make sure hems are generous, especially in expensive dresses, suits and coats. Kids tend to grow up, not out, and a couple of extra inches in length can add another year to the life of the outfit.

● Shop end-of-season clearance sales. You can pretty well guess your child's size for the following year, and you can easily save 50% by buying ahead. Try to buy things that can be adjusted if your child grows more that you anticipated. Look for loose fitting styles, elastic waists, and generous hems and cuffs.

● Buy holiday outfits at after-Christmas sales. Not only will you save at least 50%, but because you have it early, your child will be able to wear it throughout the entire season next year.

● Because you have your child's holiday outfit in advance, you can take advantage of early bird specials at portrait studios for your holiday photos.

● Shop consignment shops. Find one in a nice neighborhood. Don't shop for the cheapest things, but rather look for quality. You can pay discount-store prices and get boutique-quality clothes. This is also a good place to look for special things like ski clothes and scouting uniforms.

TOYS AND ENTERTAINMENT

● Rotate toys. Most parents know that no matter how many toys a child has, it is a good idea to keep a few of them hidden away. Then, when kids get bored, you can pull a few of them out, and they'll seem new again.

- Invest the most in toys that will last for a few years. A toy kitchen, bicycle, or sports equipment can be worth the cost because kids will use it for a long time.

Try to buy big, expensive toys at garage sales or second -hand shops.

- Buy only a few big toys and fill in with craft and art supplies. Buy these on sale at dollar and discount stores, and save them for when kids need a little entertainment. Most kids love a fresh box of glitter and glue or a new set of water colors.

- Teach kids to entertain themselves with things around the house. Kids love projects and can be entertained for hours by building a dog house, planning and preparing a family party, and planting a garden and selling the produce. If you're willing to offer support and live with the results, these projects can teach more than any toy ever will.

- Encourage kids to save up for big items like electronic games. Help them find the best price and give them some money to get started. Then offer to match or even double the money they accumulate. Not only will it save you money, but kids can learn a lot about delayed gratification.

BATH TIME

Save on novelty bath items by being inventive.

- Inexpensive shaving cream is a great bath toy. Foam some into a plastic cup and give kids a little brush to paint the shower walls. You can even mix a little food coloring into it without worrying about stains. Kids love it, and a single can will last a long time.

- When buying novelty shampoos, look for the type that you can refill with a less expensive product once the original is used up.

- Sponges in animal and other shapes are twice the cost of regular sponges. Buy cheap foam sponges and cut your own shapes.

Store bath toys in a mesh bag or plastic basket and hang it in the tub for next time.

● Tint the bath water with a drop or two of food coloring for a little excitement. You can create "pink rose water", a "blue lagoon" or a "green monster lake."

● Plastic measuring cups, spoons, and funnels can make bath time fun and educational. Kids learn to pour and estimate amounts without any mess.

● Reluctant bathers can be lured into the tub with an after dinner popsicle. Let them enjoy the drippy treat in the tub, then just wash the mess away.

● Speed things up with a shower. Some kids love it and it can save a lot of time in the evening.

● Save a little time by dressing kids in fresh underwear beneath their pajamas so they can just slip their clothes on in the morning.

FOOD

● Check the price of school lunches. In many areas it can be less expensive for children to buy lunch than to bring one from home.

● Cut the cost of juice by mixing with 1/3 to 1/2 water and serve from a pitcher.

● Individual juice packs cost a fortune. Buy your child a small canteen or sports bottle, and fill it with juice at home.

● Keep a couple of small sports bottles or sipper cups filled with juice in the refrigerator so kids can help themselves.

● Let kids make their own ice pops. Homemade juice pops are a fraction of what you pay in the store and just as good.

● Make your own fudgesicles. Kids can freeze chocolate milk in ice pop containers and save a bundle.

● Make your own chicken nuggets. Cut up chunks of chicken breast, shake in a plastic bag with a seasoned coating mix, and bake according to directions. Freeze the extras, and kids can heat their own in a microwave.

● Don't spend extra on microwave breakfasts. A quick batch of French toast or pancakes prepared on the weekend will keep in the fridge in a plastic bag for several days. Kids can reheat them in the microwave even faster than the frozen type.

Let kids pack their own snacks for a car trip. If they make their own creations, they're less likely to beg you to stop at restaurants.

● Make shape toast. On the weekend, let kids cut bread into various shapes with cookie cutters. Make them into French toast. Kids are less likely to want commercial things if homemade foods are just as much fun.

● Make your own healthy, novelty cereal. Buy store brands of basic wheat or oat cereal. Let kids add their own dried fruit and a limited amount of sugar. Make it fun by putting a small toy or surprise in a plastic bag for kids to search for. If the reward is better than what they'd get in a the commercial type, kids won't complain.

● Get kids special dishes and cups. Character dishes at meal time can make healthy food more fun and reduce the attraction to novelty food products.

Send a few crates and storage boxes. Under-the-bed storage boxes are perfect for holding their extra clothes.

OFF TO COLLEGE

*L*eaving home for college can be a confusing experience. It's almost like having to pack for a four-year trip. Because the first few weeks are stressful under the best of conditions, it's important to try to get your student's gear organized in advance. So here's a list of things he or she will need to make the transition to campus life a little easier.

● Send a hot pot. Dining halls don't stay open 24 hours a day, so a small appliance for heating snacks can be very useful.

● Send a good alarm clock that operates on both batteries and electricity. Plenty of freshmen have missed early morning classes because current or batteries have run out.

● Send a phone answering machine. This may seem like an unnecessary luxury, but it will come in handy. Students are out more than you think.

● Send a supply of stamps. They never have one when they need it, and of course they'll have time to write to their parents.

● Send boots and rain gear. A lot of first-time students forget that it rains at college, and they'll be doing a lot of walking.

● Send a shower caddy. Chances are that they'll need to tote their toiletries down the hall to the bathroom. And send along a pair of shower shoes. Institutional bathrooms aren't always as clean as the one at home.

● Check the size of bedding they'll need. Many dorm beds require extra-long sheets, and college linen services can be expensive. Buy their own and save.

● Consider buying or renting a small refrigerator. Over four years, the savings on vending machine drinks can really add up.

Buy most of their supplies at home. Bookstores and small college shops tend to be a lot more expensive.

● Make sure their bank has a branch in their college town. Parents can deposit money at home and students can easily make the withdrawal. No need to worry about a check in the mail.

● An ATM card can be a great convenience. Just be sure to get one that will work with most bank machines. This can be a lifesaver in an emergency.

● Make the students' airline reservations early. Flights around the holidays fill up fast, so get a school schedule and plan those trips early. You'll also be in a better position to get a good rate.

● Check out long-distance calling plans. Collect calls and calling cards can get expensive, so make sure your students get the best plan for your money.

● If he or she needs a computer, have him check out the prices at school. Frequently, businesses that cater to students will offer a special discount.

But even with these tips, it's going to be an expensive adventure. That's why most parents say, "My kid and my money are going to college."

Holidays

Once we have a home of our own, we realize that holidays don't happen automatically, but are created through the extra things we do. Decorating, sending cards, baking—they all combine to make holidays a special time—a little different from ordinary days. Some people observe only the major holidays, and others like to celebrate every single one. These next *Better Living* tips have been collected to help make your style of merrymaking a little easier and a lot more fun.

VALENTINE TEA

A wonderful way to celebrate Valentine's Day is with a charming Victorian custom, the Valentine Tea. Traditionally held as a short break between lunch and dinner, the entire event lasts only about an hour, requires little preparation, and is perfect for adults or children.

Because it's so quick and inexpensive, it's a great way for working moms to host something a little special without too much preparation. Here are a few tips.

● Use your best china. A tea should be a small, elegant affair where you can use your prettiest things.

● The traditional Valentine tea included an opportunity for children to make homemade Valentines. This is a nice way to keep kids occupied while adults chat. Be sure to provide plenty of supplies like paper, lace and glue.

● Traditionally, tea is served to children with great amounts of milk and a bit of sugar. It's just a little healthier and more suited to their tastes.

● Food can be elegant but simple. Cucumber sandwiches—common tea fare—are quick and inexpensive. Just cut bread with a heart-shaped cookie cutter, and spread with cream cheese and a cucumber slice.

● Scones make an authentic presentation. But you can get the same effect by cutting refrigerator biscuit dough into heart shapes. Serve them hot with strawberry jam.

Brew a pot of tea and present it with sugar, cream, and lemon slices.

Valentine cookies are perfect and can be picked up at the bakery.

● After tea, provide guests with a bit of bird seed. Tie the seed in a small bundle using nylon net and ribbon, just like the wedding packets. Folklore says that Valentine's Day is the day birds choose their mates. Guests are asked to sprinkle the seed on their way home to provide a wedding feast for the birds.

● For less than $10 and two hours' preparation time, you can turn an ordinary afternoon into a special holiday memory for your favorite Valentine.

E A S T E R   E G G   H U N T

*R*emember the fun of an old-fashioned Easter egg hunt? With more imagination than money, you can recreate this springtime memory for kids of all ages.

Hide a special egg with each child's name on it, and make it part of the fun to look for your own egg.

● Select a nice area outdoors, either in your yard or a confined area in a park. Make sure it has enough space for kids to have fun, but is not so large that it would be difficult to find the eggs.

● About an hour before guests arrive, hide candy-filled plastic eggs.

● Ask kids to bring their Easter baskets, but have a few on hand as extras.

● Hide at least six eggs per child, more if the kids are older.

● Make sure eggs are easy to spot. Finding eggs is thrilling for little ones, but they'll get frustrated if they're too hard to find.

● Let little kids go first, or designate separate areas for different age groups.

● Keep track of the eggs. Make a note of how many you hide and where you put them. This can save a lot of trouble with the lawn mower later on.

● Give prizes for finding the most eggs, the most blue eggs, even the fewest eggs. Little feelings are easily hurt, so make sure there are prizes for everyone.

Offer lots of prizes for finding specific eggs. Put a note in certain eggs to designate a prize.

● The hunt will go quickly, so for afterward plan refreshments and egg-decorating activities.

● Provide a large bowl of colored eggs and lots of craft supplies and let everyone get creative with felt, glue, magic markers, and paper.

You can dye eggs with Kool Aid®. Just mix one package of the unsweetened type with 2/3 cup warm water.

EGG DECORATING

Embellished with designs developed over generations, eggs have become the symbol of Easter. Because most of us don't have time to create works of art, egg-dyeing kits are a quick and easy way to carry on the tradition. To make things a little more interesting, though, you might like to try these few simple ideas.

● Make old-fashioned leaf and flower prints on eggs. Lay a tiny flower flat against a pastel or uncolored egg. Wrap the egg in a square of panty hose material and tie closed with a string. Lower into dye. Let the whole package dry, then cut away fabric to reveal a patterned egg.

● **Herb eggs**. Make these with the same technique as leaf and flower prints, but use fresh herbs like parsley or rosemary. They're commonly dyed a natural color like pale green and displayed in a bed of the fresh herbs.

● **Engraved eggs** are a European tradition. Just use a sharp tool like an X-Acto knife or even a pin to gently scratch a design into a dyed egg. Traditionally, eggs were engraved with a short message like "Happy Easter." Today, designs include tiny pictures, names, and dates.

● **Marbleize eggs**. Just lay a paper towel over a piece of aluminum foil. Drop 8 or 10 drops of food color (one or more colors) on the towel. Gently wrap the foil around a damp egg. Open and allow egg to dry.

● **Simple wax eggs**. Dye an egg a pale color. Use a warm wax birthday candle to write or draw a design on the egg. (Warm the candle by burning it for a few seconds, then blowing out the flame.) Then, dip the egg into the same dye or a darker color.

● Food coloring makes a great dye for eggs. Mix about a half bottle of color into 2 cups of hot water. Add 2 tablespoons vinegar and 1 tablespoon of salt, which will help establish the color. Stir and allow to cool.

● Lightly polish colored eggs with a soft cloth and a drop of vegetable oil to give them a beautiful shine.

● Use fresh, colored pasta as a nest to display eggs. Fresh pasta, which is traditionally sold in a nest shape, will dry and hold eggs securely in place for a centerpiece.

● Make an eggshell vase. Use an empty, dyed eggshell as a vase for tiny blossoms and rest it in an egg cup.

Buy extra colored grass during Easter. It's hard to find later, and you can use it for packing or gift baskets. It's a lot less expensive than the shredded tinsel sold at Christmas.

Easter Baskets

Decorated baskets, the kind that look hand-painted, cost a small fortune in the stores. But even a beginner can make them at home with fabulous results. They're perfect for Easter, but you can use the technique to make one for any special occasion. Here's how.

The technique is basically decoupage: using paper cocktail napkins and decoupage adhesive such as Mod Podge®.

A single ply of the napkin is so delicate that the adhesive will cause it to mold and shape itself over the basket weave and give a hand-painted look.

If you don't want to bother with a special decoupage medium, simple white glue, thinned with a little water, will work as well.

Start with a medium-size, painted basket. Make sure it has height on the sides to show off your design.

If you're painting the basket yourself, use acrylic spray paint. Just make sure to apply a couple of light coats to prevent drips.

Select a napkin with a beautiful design, and cut it out with sharp scissors. Cuticle scissors will help with the intricate spots.

You don't have to cut out every little notch—this technique is very forgiving. That's another reason it's so easy.

Tweezers can be handy to hold the paper when things get sticky.

You can use any design you like, but simple designs work best. Large flowers, shells, and ivy work well.

Try to select a design with the same background color as your basket. That way it won't show if you don't cut out the design perfectly.

Be sure to only use paper napkins. Other kinds of paper are too stiff for really good results.

Separate the first ply from the rest of the paper. Then arrange your pieces on a counter.

Once you're satisfied with your design, use a small brush and spread the glue on the basket, then apply the paper design. Just lightly lay it over the glued spot.

Gently go over the design with the brush, applying more glue until it's perfectly in place. Dab gently to push tiny bits of the paper into the ridges of the basket weave to give a more hand-painted look.

Don't worry about being messy. This is perfect for beginners because the glue will disappear when it dries.

Allow things to dry, then apply a few more coats for texture and to keep everything in place.

Then, to protect your work, spray with a sealant.

If you're making an Easter basket for someone special, it's a nice touch to put the date inside.

Try gluing bits of the design on the handle of the basket.

You can even let the design cascade over the top and into the basket itself.

To make the basket look more finished, glue a single flower or design in the center, inside the basket.

It's always a good idea to practice first on an old basket, but most people have good results the first time.

This technique isn't only for baskets; it can be used on wicker trays, tables, and other similar objects.

**Q
U
I
C
K

&

S
I
M
P
L
E**

Try to get a pumpkin from a pumpkin patch. Shipping does a lot of damage.

PERFECT PUMPKIN PICKING

We buy millions of pumpkins each fall, but most of us have no idea what we're paying for. Here's what you need to know before you head out to the pumpkin patch.

● There are three major varieties of pumpkins: cow pumpkins, pie pumpkins, and jack-o-lanterns.

Cow pumpkins are the common, odd-shaped variety. They're a little too wobbly for use as a jack-o-lantern, but great for roasted seeds. This variety is cheap and easy to grow, so you often find them featured in large bins at the grocery store.

Pie pumpkins are so named because they contain about 2 cups of meat, just the right amount for a pie.

Jack-o-lanterns are the best for Halloween carving. These pumpkins have lively ridges and a concave bottom so they sit well on the front porch. This type is usually the most expensive.

● Like any produce, select one that's firm and fresh looking. A good stem is attractive and can give you an indication of freshness.

● A fresh pumpkin will keep well outdoors for weeks if it doesn't freeze; but once carved, it's very perishable.

● To preserve it a little longer, spray your jack-o-lantern inside and out with a spray antiseptic.

● Rub the cut areas of the pumpkin with petroleum jelly to help protect and preserve it.

● A dried, wrinkled pumpkin can sometimes be temporarily refreshed by soaking in water.

● And don't throw seeds away. They make a great snack. Just rinse the seeds, mix with butter and seasonings and toast in the oven.

● Make a beautiful punch bowl from a hollow pumpkin by surrounding the rim with fresh flowers. Poke holes in the rim with an ice pick, place a plastic container inside to hold the punch, then fill the little holes with chrysanthemums and other Fall flowers.

Save the little munchkin pumpkins to be used as candle holders for Thanksgiving dinner.

Favorite Pumpkin Recipes

SAVANNAH SOUR CREAM PUMPKIN PIE

(The filling is as delicate and rich as a French cheese cake.)

Pie shell for a 9-inch pie
2 cups pumpkin puree, cooked, fresh, or canned
3 eggs
1 cup sour cream
1/2 cup milk
1 cup sugar
1/2 teaspoon salt
2 tablespoons bourbon
1 teaspoon cinnamon
1 teaspoon ginger
1/4 teaspoon nutmeg
1/4 teaspoon ground cloves

Prepare the crust. Our technique will give you a beautiful, flaky crust even on the bottom.

Preheat oven to 450 degrees. Place the crust in a 9-inch pie pan and prick all over with a fork. Press a piece of heavy-duty foil directly into the pie shell. Bake for 6 minutes, then remove the foil. Return to the oven and bake for 4 more minutes. Remove and set aside.

In a large bowl, beat pumpkin, eggs, sour cream, milk, and sugar. Add salt, bourbon, cinnamon, ginger, nutmeg, and cloves. Beat until smooth.

Pour filling into the pie shell and bake for 10 minutes.

Reduce heat to 300 degrees, and continue to bake for 30 to 40 minutes or until the filling is almost firm.

Serve plain, or topped with whipped cream and a sprinkle of pecans.

OLD-FASHIONED PUMPKIN SEEDS

2 cups seeds
1 1/2 tablespoons butter or oil
1 1/4 teaspoons salt
1/4 teaspoon garlic powder (optional)

Rinse seeds until clean, being careful to remove strings. Spread on an absorbent cloth and pat dry. Toss with butter or oil, salt, and garlic powder. Spread on an ungreased cookie sheet. Bake at 250 degrees until golden brown. Baking time varies on how crisp you want the seeds. The longer you bake them, the crisper they will be. Begin checking after 15 minutes. They can bake as long as an hour.

Pumpkin Carving Secrets

*W*hether you call them pumpkin heads, jack-o-lanterns or pumpkin moonshines, they're a wonderful form of American folk art. And just as with other crafts, there are a few clever tricks that will make your pumpkin carving a glowing success.

Draw your design on paper. Markers and pencils don't work very well on pumpkin skin. Pin the design to the pumpkin with straight pins.

● First, select a pumpkin with a smooth skin. It will be easier to create a design on it.

● To get started, draw a lid on the top of your pumpkin. Remove the top if you plan to light it with a candle; remove the bottom if you plan to set the pumpkin over an electric light.

● Make a little notch in the pumpkin where you cut off the lid. This way you can line the lid up with the pumpkin for a perfect fit.

● Then scoop out your pumpkin. Using a flat spoon or scoop, scrape away the inside meat so the shell is only about 1 inch thick. This will make carving a lot easier.

● Now, using a push pin, begin perforating your design. Once the design has been marked, go back and poke the holes all the way through with an ice pick or some other poking tool.

● Next, it's basically a matter of connecting the dots. Use a thin serrated knife or pumpkin saw. You can buy inexpensive pumpkin-carving tools that are wonderful and make carving a lot easier.

● If you have trouble seeing the holes, dust your design with flour and they'll show up better.

● Saw, don't slice. An up-and-down sawing motion is much easier to control.

A star-shaped cookie cutter makes a good template for a wizard design.

● Be creative with your designs; they don't all have to be faces.

● Create a stained glass pumpkin by pinning colorful flame-resistant gel or paper inside. A simple design of squares or triangles will create an extraordinary effect.

● The last step is to create a chimney. Light the candle inside your completed pumpkin, and allow it to burn for a minute. Then, check the lid for smoke marks. Cut an opening in the spot where the smoke naturally rises, and your candle should burn nicely.

HALLOWEEN SCAVENGER HUNT

*I*t's an eerie thought, but Halloween has become one of America's favorite holidays. Why not create a creepy and fun experience for little ones with a back yard Halloween Scavenger Hunt?

Supply kids with large bags and send them off to search for spooky things you've hidden in advance.

● For atmosphere, fill trees with ghosts by hanging white plastic bags over balloons. Add a few cobwebs and pumpkins to make things creepier.

● Novelty shops and dollar stores are great places to pick up inexpensive supplies.

● Give older kids a list of items to collect, or if some children are too young to read, make a poster-size picture board of everything the explorers need to bring back.

● Kids will love looking for inexpensive trinkets such as rubber spiders hidden behind bushes and trees. Be careful not to hide things too well.

● Create an instant pumpkin patch in a bed of pine straw. Buy several small pumpkins and lay them out in rows. Make the patch more fun by building a scarecrow. Have each child wander through the patch looking for a specific pumpkin with his or her name written on the bottom.

● Next, kids are off to the haystack to sift through straw looking for a small novelty to help complete their scavenger collection. This is always a huge hit. Kids love to jump and dig in the hay. Have one or two bales delivered by your garden center.

● The last item on the hunt is an apple. Of course, the only way they can get one is to bob for it in a big tub of water. Have towels on hand for drippy faces.

● The reward for all this is a Witch's Feast. Serve your favorite Halloween goodies.

● Let kids take home all the items they collected for the scavenger hunt as party favors.

HALLOWEEN FUN

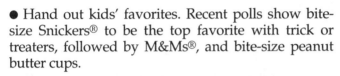alloween is a great time for neighbors to team up to make it a fun event for kids and adults. Here are a few tips for celebrating the creepiest night of the year.

Masks can be dangerous for small children. Instead try a little creative makeup.

● Hand out kids' favorites. Recent polls show bite-size Snickers® to be the top favorite with trick or treaters, followed by M&Ms®, and bite-size peanut butter cups.

● Include parents in the fun by offering special adult treats like hot cider or coffee in a paper cup. A tray of Halloween cookies or a little bag of popcorn to munch along the way will make things more fun for everyone.

● Have an instant camera ready. Snap a photo of the little goblins who come to your door, and send it home as a special treat.

● For safety reasons, most parents prefer that you offer only wrapped candy, but you can make a few special homemade treats for people you know well. It's a fun activity to do with your own kids to help get them in the spirit.

● For quick sideburns, moustache or beard, use a moist sponge to apply cake mascara, eyeliner or dark eye shadow.

● Chalk mixed with shortening can be applied for ghost makeup.

● Strands of spaghetti, sprayed or colored black with a magic marker, make perfect animal whiskers.

● Make realistic bruises by mixing lipstick with yellow eye shadow.

Create lots of miniature jack-o-lanterns by drawing faces on oranges with magic marker.

● To remove make up, use baby shampoo. It can be much less abrasive to tender skin.

● Make your house a fun experience. Because most kids can only visit a few neighbors, try to add a little Halloween atmosphere to their visit. Lights, pumpkins, ghosts, and witches all add up to create the chills kids will remember for a lifetime.

● For adult fun, invite a few friends to enjoy one of the ancient traditions of Halloween, apple fortunes.

A P P L E   F O R T U N E S

Cut an apple in half from top to bottom. Choose one half and count the number of seeds.

One Seed   Next year will be pretty much the same as this one.

Two seeds   You'll be lucky in love.

Three seeds   You can expect a financial windfall.

Four seeds   You'll take a long trip.

Five Seeds   You'll be very happy in your work for the next year.

Six seeds   You'll experience good health.

Seven seeds   All of life's blessings are yours next year.

THANKSGIVING TIME AND MONEY SAVERS

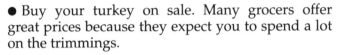he fun of one of America's favorite holidays can be spoiled by the time and money spent preparing the meal. Here are a few *Better Living* tips to cut down on both.

Buy rolls and stuffing cubes at bakery thrift shops. You'll save about 50%.

● Buy your turkey on sale. Many grocers offer great prices because they expect you to spend a lot on the trimmings.

● A plain turkey is usually less expensive and healthier than the self-basting type. Basically you're paying extra for extra fat.

● Plan on 1 pound of turkey per person when buying a bird 12 pounds or smaller; with a larger bird, 3/4 of a pound should be enough.

● To save kitchen space, thaw a frozen turkey in a picnic cooler placed in the bathtub. Use the running water technique.

● Chop and freeze vegetables like onions and celery for stuffing ahead of time. Then just dump them in with other ingredients when you are ready to prepare the stuffing.

● Plan your linens and decorations ahead. Don't bother ironing the tablecloth, a quick touch-up while it's on the table is usually sufficient.

● Make starter gravy cubes in advance. Mix flour and water and freeze in ice cube trays. Then pop them into turkey drippings and stir. For a very rich gravy some people like to freeze equal parts of flour and whipped butter.

Organize your serving pieces in advance. Plan to microwave frozen vegetables in their serving bowls.

● Freeze cranberries before grinding or chopping. It will be much neater whether you're making cranberry sauce or adding them to baked goods.

● Tiny pumpkins, squash, or apples make great candle holders. Just carve a hole in the top for the candle. Set them on a small bed of dried leaves for a natural centerpiece.

● Don't peel potatoes. Unpeeled potatoes make delicious, attractive mashed potatoes. Just wash and trim thoroughly, boil, and mash as usual.

● Add a teaspoon or so of baking soda to mashed potatoes to make them very light and fluffy.

● You can even make mashed potatoes ahead for a large crowd. Prepare them as usual, adding a little extra milk. Then keep them warm and moist in an electric crock pot set on low.

● Make pumpkin pies in advance and freeze unbaked. Prevent a soggy crust by buttering the bottom of the pie pan.

● To protect crust from burning, fold a square of aluminum foil into fourths. Cut a wedge shape from the middle, then unfold.You should have a round hole in the middle. Fit the whole thing over the pie so that only the edges of the crust are covered. Remove for the last few minutes of baking.

● Turkey-shaped cookies, store bought or homemade in advance, make great place cards. Pipe guests' names on cookies and place on each dinner plate.

TURKEY TIPS

*E*very Thanksgiving, millions of turkeys end up as the star attraction on American dinner tables. But the most important one is yours. So let's talk turkey. Here's what you need to know.

Look for the USDA inspection mark to be sure it's been inspected and accurately labeled.

Look for the age category on the label. The younger the bird, the more tender it will be. A young turkey is usually 4-6 months of age.

Due to special food processing technology, fresh turkey now has a relatively long shelf life and can be purchased ahead.

If you prefer frozen, don't select a turkey that's stacked above the store's freezer case. It may have begun to thaw.

If you're preparing a turkey breast, then 3/4 of a pound per person should be enough.

To thaw your turkey in the refrigerator takes planning; allow about 24 hours for every 5 pounds.

The cold water thawing method is quicker. Submerge the fully wrapped bird; about 5 hours for a small bird and 12 hours for the larger ones. Be sure to change the water every 30 minutes.

Remember to remove neck and giblets from the body cavity.

Wash the bird thoroughly, inside and out.

Allow 3/4 of a cup of stuffing per pound of turkey. Be sure to stuff lightly because stuffing expands as it cooks.

Place the bird in a shallow roasting pan, breast side up. Don't add water.

Brush the entire bird with a little oil or melted margarine to give it a golden brown color.

Cover the turkey very loosely with a tent made of aluminum foil. This will help keep the bird moist.

Pop the bird into a 325 degree oven and that's it. A few hours later, depending on the size, you should have a gorgeous, golden brown bird.

Allow it to sit 1 minute per pound before carving. This will give the juices time to settle, and the meat time to become firm enough for slicing.

For a little more of a gourmet technique, sprinkle the bird with chopped fresh herbs such as sage and thyme; then wrap it completely in foil or a clear cooking bag and roast.

Garnish the platter with sprigs of fresh herbs and small fruits, like grapes or cranberries, for an elegant presentation.

Surround the turkey with mashed potato rosettes made in advance and frozen. Then on the big day, brush with butter and bake. (See recipe on next page)

T U R K E Y   T I M E T A B L E

Weight	Stuffed	Unstuffed
6-8 lbs.	3 to 3 1/2 hrs.	2 1/2 to 3 1/2 hrs.
8-12 lbs.	3 1/2 to 4 1/2 hrs.	3 to 4 hrs.
12-16 lbs.	4 to 5 hrs.	3 1/2 to 4 1/2 hrs.
16-20 lbs	4 1/2 to 5 1/2 hrs.	4 to 5 hrs.

Approximate roasting times for thawed turkey at 325 degrees in a conventional oven.

POTATO ROSETTES

3 medium potatoes
margarine
about 2 tablespoons milk
salt and pepper
1 egg

Prepare potatoes as you would mashed potatoes. Allow to cool slightly. Add egg and blend at low speed with an electric mixer. Place mixture in a pastry bag. Pipe into rosettes on a cookie sheet. Freeze. Remove from cookie sheet and store in a zip-lock freezer bag.

To bake, place frozen rosettes on a lightly greased cookie sheet. Lightly brush with butter or margarine. Bake at 325 degrees for about 25 minutes or until heated and slightly golden.

Save on postage by mailing Christmas post cards instead of traditional greeting cards.

HOLIDAY BUDGET TIPS

'Tis the season to overspend, and not just on gifts. Some things are obvious, but there can be hundreds of hidden holiday expenses. Financial experts tell us that this is the time of year when lots of people go overboard, often without realizing it. So here are a few ways to help you stick to your budget.

● Set a limit. Know how much you have to spend, then decide what you want to spend it on. Cut corners on the things that are least important to you.

● Get everything out of the attic and do an inventory of your holiday items. This way you won't buy extra candles, bulbs, and other things you don't really need.

● Don't spend money on lots of new gift wrap. Inventory what you already have, then gather things from around the house that you can use.

● Remember that a lot of paper and ribbon can be refreshed by ironing.

● Instead of buying individual gifts at the office, be the first to take in holiday goodies. Attach a little tag so everyone will know who brought the gift.

● Don't go overboard on entertaining. Plan parties after mealtime and serve only desert and coffee. It can still be elegant and festive. You'll save time, too.

For large families or groups, encourage a Pollyanna type gift exchange with a price limit.

● Busy schedules mean last-minute meals. Plan quick and easy meals ahead of time to avoid expensive take-out at the last minute.

● Plan holiday travel carefully to avoid overspending. This includes extra trips for shopping as well as a travel to visit family.

HOLIDAY SPENDING PLAN

Planning ahead is the best way to avoid overspending during the holidays. This handy form will help you to anticipate the seasonal expenses that can destroy your budget.

Keep track of seasonal spending. Develop a holiday budget and stick to it.

GIFTS

Name	Gift	Estimate	Cost
____	____	____	____
____	____	____	____
____	____	____	____
____	____	____	____
____	____	____	____
____	____	____	____
____	____	____	____
____	____	____	____
____	____	____	____
____	____	____	____
____	____	____	____
____	____	____	____
____	____	____	____

GIFTS: Charities, Donations, Office Collections, Etc.

____	____	____	____
____	____	____	____
____	____	____	____
____	____	____	____
____	____	____	____
____	____	____	____

GIFT WRAP

	Estimate	Cost
Gift boxes	____	____
Paper	____	____
Bows, tags, tape	____	____
Novelty attachments	____	____
Professional gift-wrapping	____	____
Number of gifts___ at $____/gift	____	____
Heavy paper, tubes, boxes, twine, labels, tape	____	____
Other	____	____

HOLIDAY GREETINGS

	Estimate	Cost
Greeting cards	___	___
Photo inserts	___	___
Holiday newsletter	___	___
Long distance calls	___	___

POSTAGE AND FREIGHT

Cards
Number of cards___ at $____/card ___ ___
Packages to be sent
Number of pkgs.___at $____/pkg. ___ ___
Other ___ ___

SUBTOTAL #1 ___ ___

PICTURES

Film
Number of rolls___at $____/roll ___ ___
Developing
Number of rolls___at $____/roll ___ ___

DECORATING

Christmas tree and stand	___	___
Tree decorations	___	___
Household decorations	___	___
Greenery (wreaths, garland)	___	___
Candles	___	___
Fresh and/or artificial flowers	___	___
Outdoor decorations	___	___
Outdoor lighting	___	___
Other	___	___

TRAVEL

	Estimate	Cost
Gas for errands, around-town trips	____	____
Bus fares for errands	____	____
Long-distance travel	____	____
Mileage or airfare	____	____
Meals on the road	____	____
Lodging	____	____
Miscellaneous	____	____
Other	____	____

HOLIDAY BAKING

Staples (flour, sugar, etc.)	____	____
Special ingredients	____	____
Equipment (cookie sheets, pans)	____	____

ENTERTAINING

Entertaining others
    Function_____

Food cost	____	____
Beverage cost	____	____
Invitations and postage	____	____
Miscellaneous	____	____
Other	____	____

Being entertained
    Hostess gifts   ____ ____

Baby sitting
    Number of days/nights __at $__ ____ ____

New clothes	____	____
Dry cleaning	____	____
SUBTOTAL #2	____	____

MISCELLANEOUS

	Estimate	*Cost*
Meals eaten in restaurants		
Number of meals__at $___/meal	_____	_____
Seasonal albums and tapes	_____	_____
Movie, play & concert admissions	_____	_____
Professional housecleaning	_____	_____
Professional carpet cleaning	_____	_____
Other_____	_____	_____
Other_____	_____	_____
Other_____	_____	_____
SUBTOTAL #3	_____	_____

SUBTOTAL #1   _____   _____

SUBTOTAL #2   _____   _____

SUBTOTAL #3   _____   _____

TOTAL HOLIDAY EXPENDITURES _____   _____

*Note: This holiday spending plan was developed by
Virginia Cooperative Extension*

CHRISTMAS TREES

*F*or a lot of us, the house wouldn't feel like Christmas without a fresh tree. The tradition may have stayed the same, but a lot has changed in the Christmas tree business. There are more varieties than ever to choose from. Here's what you need to know.

Make sure the tree is brightly colored and has a robust fragrance.

PINE TREES

If you like to leave your tree up for a long time, White or Scotch pines have great staying power.

Pine trees are very fragrant and have long needles that will stay on the branches for quite awhile.

Pines have very sharp needles, and decorating can be a very prickly experience, especially for small children.

SPRUCE TREES

Spruce trees have that rustic Rocky Mountain Christmas look. They are very full, with bristly needles all around.

They're beautiful, but when they dry out, they drop their needles instantly.

FIR TREES

If your family has collected lots of heavy ornaments over the years, a fir tree might be a good choice. They have very soft, flexible needles, a nice fragrance, and can support heavy ornaments.

Firs, such as Douglas or Frasier, have become popular over the last few years but tend to be more expensive than pine or spruce.

Instead of using water, avoid spills by filling the tree stand with ice cubes, which can water the tree as they melt.

● All trees, no matter how fresh, continually drop needles from the inside branches.

● Test for freshness only on the outside. Grasp a branch about six inches in and pull lightly along the branch to make sure needles are firmly attached.

● A sap seal forms over the trunk after harvesting, so be sure to cut about an inch off the trunk to allow the tree to take in moisture.

● A tree can actually take in a gallon of water in the first 24 hours, so place it in a bucket of warm water as soon as you get it home.

● Set your tree up away from heat sources and close any nearby air vents. Try to keep the tree as cool as possible.

● Keep water in the tree stand throughout the season.

● No matter which variety you choose, make sure the tree is fresh.

CHRISTMAS TIPS

*F*or most of us, holiday time is the busiest time of the year. It takes lots of organization to keep things running smoothly, so here are a few *Better Living* tips to make the season a little simpler.

● Put Christmas lights on timers to save the trouble of turning them on and off every night.

● Don't use the same strings of lights year after year. Even though the lights work, the plastic covering can dry out and crack, and become a fire hazard.

● When you're buying batteries for toys, be sure to buy fresh ones for your smoke alarm, too. Make it a holiday tradition to replace them.

● To keep pine sap from damaging tablecloths and wood surfaces, just seal off the ends of the boughs with a dab of glue or a dip in liquid paraffin.

● Spray holiday linens in advance with a spray-on fabric protector to prevent stains from candle wax and other seasonal spills.

● Protect trees and decorations from kids and pets by hanging warning bells near the bottom. That way you'll know when little ones get too close.

● When ordering Christmas gifts by mail, write all the information about your order right on the check. That way, if you have a problem, you'll have a complete record.

● Protect delicate Christmas ornaments by storing them individually in old socks.

● Spray candle holders with vegetable spray to make wax easier to remove.

● Save your wrapping paper tubes and use them to store tree lights. Just wrap each light string around a tube and tuck the plug inside.

● A tall waste paper basket makes a perfect place to store holiday gift wrap.

CHRISTMAS COOKIE COLLECTION

*C*ookies are among the most fun, most appreciated, and least expensive ways to celebrate the holidays. Nothing is more evocative of childhood memories than the taste and smell of favorite family cookie recipes. A few secrets, collected from world-class cookie bakers, can make creating these sweets quick and easy. No matter what recipe you use, here are some great tips that can help make even your very first batch a big success.

A buttered cookie sheet will cause cookies to change shape. Grease with oil or cooking spray instead.

● The ideal cookie sheet is 2 to 3 inches shorter than your oven so that the heating element can brown things evenly. The cookie sheet should be made of shiny, heavy gauged aluminum.

● Make bar cookies in a foil-lined, glass pan so they can be lifted out and cut evenly—no squashed edges.

● Slice-and-bake cookie rolls should be rotated a quarter turn after each slice to prevent one side from getting flat.

● Roll out cookie dough on a lightly floured pillowcase. It's the perfect size, and the fabric will prevent the cookie dough from sticking.

● When rolling cookie dough, dust with powdered sugar instead of flour. It prevents dough from sticking, but won't make it tough the way flour does. You may prefer a blend of one part powdered sugar and one part flour, if you tend to incorporate a lot into the dough.

Always use large size eggs because recipes are created with this size in mind.

● Eggs should be separated when cold and then allowed to come to room temperature before being added to a baking recipe. This will give the recipe better volume.

To keep frosting moist and prevent it from cracking, beat in a pinch of baking soda.

● Try to make cookies a uniform size so they will bake evenly.

● Butter in the recipe will yield a crisp cookie; oil in the recipe will make the cookies softer and more tender.

● Baking sheets without sides give best results because sides can trap heat and moisture. If using sheets with sides, turn them upside-down and bake on the bottom.

● Make sure cookie dough is well chilled before rolling. If it becomes too cold to handle easily, allow it to stand at room temperature for a few minutes.

● Use superfine sugar to keep cookies from cracking. You can make your own by placing granulated sugar in a food processor and blending until it is very fine.

● Dip intricate cookie cutters in warm vegetable oil before cutting to allow for more defined impressions in the dough. This is especially important with plastic cookie cutters.

● Make your own brown sugar by adding molasses to ordinary white sugar. The more molasses, the darker the sugar.

● A carrot makes a good cookie press. Cut a design in the end of a large carrot, and press on a ball of cookie dough to flatten before baking.

● Give cookies an elegant, gilded look by brushing them with edible gold dust mixed with a tiny drop of water or vodka. You can buy this in specialty shops or craft stores with cake decorating sections.

Do not store crisp and soft cookies together. It will cause the crisp ones to soften as well.

● To add bright colors to cookies, paint with egg tempera. Mix egg yolks with food color and brush on before baking. You may add a tiny drop of water for consistency.

● Make your own colored sugar by shaking a little granulated sugar and a few drops of food color in a zip-lock bag.

- To prepare cookies for hanging, cut a hole with a soda straw before baking. Once removed from the oven, slip a ribbon through the hole.

- Freeze frosted cookies unwrapped on a baking sheet for 2 hours so that frosting won't be sticky when you wrap them for storage in the freezer.

- Recrisp cookies by heating for about 5 minutes in a 250 degree oven.

To retain shapes and impressions on cut out cookies, chill before baking.

Better Living's *Most Requested Holiday Cookie Recipes*

SUPER SHAPE SUGAR COOKIES
(The best recipe for using cookie cutters)

3 1/2 cups flour
2 1/2 teaspoons baking powder
3/4 teaspoon salt
1 cup butter or margarine
1 2/3 cups sugar
2 eggs
1 tablespoon vanilla extract

Combine first three ingredients and set aside. Cream butter or margarine and sugar until light and fluffy. Add eggs and vanilla, beating well. Stir in dry ingredients.

Shape dough into a log and wrap in plastic wrap. Chill in the refrigerator for about an hour.

Flour your work surface, rolling pin, and inside of cookie cutter so that dough does not stick.

For shaped cookies, roll out a small amount of dough about 1/4 inch thick and cut with a cookie cutter. Bake in moderate oven (350 degrees) for 8 to 10 minutes. Remove and transfer to wire rack to cool. Frost or sprinkle with powdered or colored sugar.

TIP—If dough is sticky, liberally sprinkle your work surface with a blend of powdered sugar and flour. Gently work dough to incorporate enough of the flour mixture to make dough easy to handle.

LADY LOCKS

A small tube of puff pastry, perfect for filling.
Delicate and impressive

1 package prepared puff pastry
(found in grocery store freezer case)
Round clothespins
Aluminum foil

Wrap round-type clothespins in a square of aluminum foil. Be sure to wrap smoothly and twist each end very tightly (remember you'll need to remove the lady lock by sliding it off).

Roll dough lightly on a counter sprinkled with flour.

Cut it into several 1-inch-wide strips about 6 inches long.

Working quickly to prevent the dough from getting too warm, spiral each strip around a clothespin to create a tube or "lady lock."

Place on ungreased cookie sheet with end piece down. This prevents it from popping loose during baking.

Bake according to package directions until golden brown.

After baking, while it's still hot, gently slide lady lock off clothespin.

TIP—A light coat of vegetable spray on the foil will help the lady lock slide off more easily after baking.

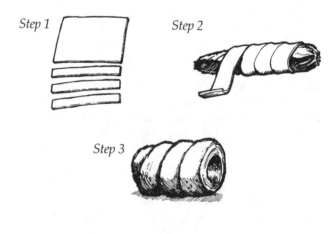

Step 1

Step 2

Step 3

LADY LOCK CREAM FILLING

4 tablespoons flour
1 cup milk
2 cups solid white shortening, such as Crisco®
2 cups powdered sugar
3/4 cup marshmallow cream
1 teaspoon vanilla

Mix flour and milk in a saucepan, on stove, stirring constantly until it forms a paste. Remove from heat and cool.

While mixture is cooling, mix other ingredients together, add flour mixture and beat.

Lightly tint cream with food coloring if you like.

Use a pastry bag to fill lady lock shells, (or you can use a plastic zip-lock bag, with one corner snipped off, in place of the pastry bag).

PATTY PIES

Super simple and impressive

1 package brownie mix
Small chocolate peanut butter cup candies
Foil cups for tart pans (approximately 1 to 1 1/2 inches in diameter)

Prepare brownie mix according to directions for "chewy" consistency.

Spoon into tart pans lined with foil cups.

Fill 3/4 full.

Push a peanut butter cup down into batter of each tart, about 3/4 of the way down.

Bake at temperature recommended on package directions (approximately 15 minutes.)

C R A N B E R R Y   W I N K S

Hearty and delicious

1 cup flour
1 teaspoon baking powder
1/2 teaspoon ground cinnamon
1/4 teaspoon nutmeg
1/2 cup butter or margarine
2/3 cup packed brown sugar
1 egg
1/4 cup milk
1 teaspoon finely shredded orange peel
1 1/2 cups quick-cooking rolled oats
3/4 cup chopped cranberries
1/4 cup chopped walnuts
orange frosting

Stir together flour, baking powder, cinnamon, and nutmeg, and set aside. In a large bowl, beat butter or margarine until softened. Add brown sugar and beat until fluffy. Mix in egg, milk, and orange peel, and beat well. Add flour mixture and beat until well mixed. Stir in oats, cranberries, and nuts.

Drop by rounded tablespoons on to a greased cookie sheet.

Bake at 375 degrees for 10 to 12 minutes.

Remove to a wire rack to cool.

Dip tops of cookies in orange frosting.

....

O R A N G E   F R O S T I N G

1 cup powdered sugar
1/2 teaspoon finely shredded orange peel
1/4 teaspoon vanilla
1 to 2 tablespoons orange juice

Stir first three ingredients together. Begin adding orange juice until frosting reaches a consistency thin enough to dip cookies in.

SOUR CREAM CHOCOLATE CHIP COOKIES

A cut above the ordinary

1 1/2 cups sugar
1/2 cup sour cream
1/4 cup margarine or butter, softened
1/4 cup shortening
1 teaspoon vanilla
1 egg
2 1/4 cups flour
1/2 teaspoon baking soda
1/4 teaspoon salt
1 package chocolate chips (milk or semi-sweet)

Heat oven to 350 degrees. Mix sugar, sour cream, margarine, shortening, vanilla, and egg in large bowl. Stir in all other ingredients except chips. Stir in chocolate chips.

Drop by rounded teaspoonfuls about 2 inches apart onto ungreased cookie sheet. Bake 12 to 14 minutes or until set and just beginning to brown. Cool on cookie sheet till lightly set.

CHOCOLATE CRUNCHERS

A light bar cookie with a crunchy meringue topping

4 tablespoons shortening or butter
1/4 teaspoon salt
1/2 cup brown sugar
1/2 teaspoon baking powder
1 egg
1 cup chocolate chips
1/2 teaspoon vanilla extract
3/4 cup flour

Preheat oven to 325 degrees.

Grease an 8-inch square baking pan.

Combine shortening or butter and brown sugar. Cream together. Add egg and vanilla, then beat.

Mix flour, salt and baking powder and add them to the first mixture. Beat until completely blended.

Stir in chocolate chips.

Spread mixture evenly in the baking pan.

MERINGUE TOPPING

1/2 cup brown sugar
1 egg white
1/2 cup chopped nuts

Beat egg white until it stands in stiff peaks; continue beating and gradually add the 1/2 cup brown sugar. Sugar will not dissolve completely. Fold in nuts.

Spread meringue evenly over the batter and bake for 25 minutes. The top will be slightly cracked and a golden brown.

Cool on a rack and then cut into 2-inch squares.

COCONUT SNOWFLAKES

3/4 cup butter or margarine
1 egg
1/2 cup sugar
2 1/4 cups flour
1/2 teaspoon vanilla
1/2 teaspoon almond extract
2 1/3 cups flaked coconut
half-and-half

Cream butter and sugar with electric mixer till fluffy. Add egg and blend. Gradually add flour until fully blended. Add vanilla, almond extract and 1 1/3 cups coconut.

Divide dough in half and wrap in waxed paper. Chill for 30 minutes.

Remove from refrigerator and quickly roll out to approximately 1/8 inch thick.

Brush dough with half-and-half and sprinkle with the remaining coconut.

Cut into shapes and bake at 400 degrees for about 6 minutes.

F R U I T   S L I C E S

Light and elegant

1 cup butter or margarine, softened
1 cup sugar
2 eggs
1 1/2 teaspoons vanilla
3 cups all-purpose flour
1 teaspoon salt
Food colors (green, yellow and red)
1 1/2 teaspoons lemon peel, grated
1 1/2 teaspoons lime peel, grated
1 1/2 teaspoons orange peel, grated
Colored sugars (yellow, orange, and green)

Mix together butter, plain sugar, eggs, and vanilla. Blend in salt and flour. Divide dough into 4 equal parts.

To one section of the dough, add a few drops of yellow food color and the lemon peel. To another section of the dough, add a few drops of green food color and the lime peel. And to another section, add a few drops each of red and yellow food color and the orange peel to make an orange color. Leave the fourth section of the dough plain. Cover and chill for 1 hour.

Shape each color dough into a roll, 2 inches in diameter and 4 inches long. Divide plain dough into 3 equal parts. Roll each part into a rectangle, 6x4 inches. Wrap 1 rectangle around each roll of colored dough. Press together firmly. Roll each roll of dough in matching colored sugar. Wrap and chill for at least 4 hours.

Heat oven to 400 degrees. Cut rolls into 1/8 inch slices. Next, cut slices in half. Place on ungreased baking sheet. Bake 6 to 8 minutes or just until set. Immediately remove from baking sheet.

S A N T A ' S   S U G A R   P L U M S

1/2 cup (1 stick) softened butter or margarine
3/4 cup confectioner's sugar
1 tablespoon vanilla
Food color to make colored dough (optional)
1 1/2 cups all-purpose flour
1/8 teaspoon salt
Dates, M&Ms®, nuts, morsels, maraschino cherries, jellybeans or other small candies or sweets.
Colored sugars

Heat oven to 350 degrees. Mix together butter, vanilla, and confectioner's sugar (at this point add a few drops of food coloring if desired). Work in flour and salt until dough holds together (if dough is dry, mix in 1 to 2 tablespoons of half and half. If dough is too sticky, mix in 1 to 2 tablespoons of flour).

Wrap 1 tablespoon of dough around nuts or candies and form into a small ball shape. Place cookies about l inch apart on ungreased baking sheet. Bake 12 to 15 minutes or until set but not brown. Let cool, then dip cookie tops in icing, and sprinkle lightly with colored sugar or other decorations.

....

I C I N G

Mix 1 cup confectioner's sugar, 2 1/2 tablespoons half-and-half, and 1 teaspoon vanilla until smooth and creamy. If desired, stir in a few drops of food color. These cookies are especially lovely when frosted with pastel shades.

....

C H O C O L A T E   I C I N G

Use same recipe as above but increase half-and-half to 3 tablespoons and stir in 1 ounce of melted, unsweetened chocolate. Be sure the chocolate is melted, but cool.

POINSETTIA COOKIES

Very impressive

3/4 *cup margarine or butter, softened*
1 *egg*
1/2 *cup sugar*
1-3 *oz. package cream cheese*
1 *teaspoon vanilla*
2 *cups all-purpose flour*
Red food color
Green candy pieces
Yellow nonpareils

Mix margarine, sugar, vanilla, food color, egg, and cream cheese in large bowl. Stir in flour. Cover and refrigerate dough about 2 hours or until firm.

(NOTE: A vivid red color takes approximately 1/3 to 1/2 of a small bottle of food coloring.)

Heat oven to 375 degrees. Roll dough into 1 1/4 inch balls. Place about 2 inches apart on ungreased cookie sheet. Using a lightly floured paring knife, cut 6 wedges about three-fourths of the way down through dough. Spread wedges slightly apart (cookies will flatten as they bake). Bake 10 to 12 minutes or until set and edges begin to brown. When cookies are still warm, press a small piece of green candy into center of cookie. After a few seconds, sprinkle yellow beads onto the melted candy center. Carefully remove from cookie sheet and cool.

Makes about 3 dozen cookies.

Let little ones string colorful Lifesavers on ribbon. Tie a bow and hang it on the tree.

CHRISTMAS DECORATING TIPS

*D*ecorations are a big part of holiday fun, but they can take up a lot of valuable time and money. Here are few ideas to make decking the halls a little easier and cheaper.

● Always buy shorter strands of tree lights. If a string goes out, it will be less noticeable, not to mention cheaper and easier to replace.

● Store lights on artificial trees. If you have an artificial tree, put lights on each section. After the holidays, take the sections apart and store separately with lights still in place. Next year's tree assembly will be a snap!

● Wrap gifts as you go along. Set up a wrapping station in an out-of-the-way place. Keep gifts nearby in a laundry basket and wrap one or two when you have a few spare minutes.

● Make inexpensive decorations with a can of gold paint. Spray paint baskets, candles, nuts, leaves, flower pots or other objects and arrange them into a display. For example, a basket of gold nuts and pine cones looks elegant and costs pennies. Paint may not cover item completely after the first coat. Be patient and spray lightly several times to avoid drips.

Glittered fresh fruit will last from one to three weeks. Of course, it's not edible.

● A little glitter and glue can turn real or plastic fruit into a sparkling centerpiece. Lightly rub fruit with a small piece of wax paper dipped in glue. Roll gently in glitter and set aside on newspaper or wax paper to dry overnight. A pint of glue and a medium-size carton of glitter will cover about a dozen pieces of fruit.

● Ice cream cone ornaments are fun to make with kids. Just let them glue plain Christmas balls onto real ice cream cones. Satin covered styrofoam balls are safer for children to work with.

● Make a teddy bear garland by tracing a teddy bear cookie cutter on a strip of grocery bag folded "paper doll fashion." Unfold the garland and draw faces and sweaters on each bear with colored markers. It's fun to write the name of each family member on the bears. Use garland to trim the tree.

● Make a colorful gumdrop tree with a styrofoam cone, toothpicks, and gumdrops. Break toothpicks in half. With a gumdrop secured to one end, poke the toothpick into the cone. Even very little children can help with this.

Make a candy garland by stapling together wrapped hard candies. Drape it on the tree or wrap it around pine garland for added color.

Lottery tickets make fun stocking stuffers.

GIFT SHOPPING TIME SAVERS

Christmas is generally the time we all rack our brains trying to come up with clever gift ideas—not to mention gifts that are reasonably priced and easy to shop for. So here are a few time and money-saving ideas that might help make Santa's shopping a little easier.

● Buy everyone the same thing. Shopping in one place, such as a music store or a book shop, can really save time.

● Buy subscriptions to everyone's favorite magazines. Everyone on your list will think of you all year long.

● Give a book of stamps and a box of all-occasion cards or stationery.

● Restaurant gift certificates make great family gifts. You can buy them at first-class restaurants, fast-food places, or anything in between.

● The drug store is a much less crowded place to buy everything from small appliances, perfume, cosmetics, toys, to wrapping paper.

● Give gift certificates for maid service or a car wash.

● Plan a midnight shopping trip. Shop in stores open 24 hours, to avoid holiday crowds and traffic.

Give movie passes. Place them in a popcorn box under the tree for a great gift.

● Shop catalogs early. Just like stores, they can run out of popular merchandise.

● Give long-distance phone certificates to family and friends who live out of town.

● Buy savings bonds or shares of stock for the young ones on your list. Show them how to follow their investment's progress.

WRAP IT UP

*S*ometimes gift wrap can cost more than the gift itself. But with a few inexpensive supplies, you can create the most beautiful packages under the tree without spending a fortune. Here are a few suggestions.

Let little children decorate their own gifts by covering plain wrapped packages with lots of sticky stars.

● Save money by purchasing paper and ribbons in solid colors and adding decorations to give them a holiday look. That way you can use the same paper throughout the year for other occasions. You'll also have the added benefit of needing to store less gift wrap.

● Collect things throughout the year to use as package decorations. You may find you've collected enough ribbons, flowers, and doodads that you won't need to buy any.

● Wrap up a gift to look like a chocolate kiss. Place the gift on a sturdy paper plate or cardboard circle. Fold a large sheet of aluminum foil up around the gift to create the shape. Make the tag out of a long strip of white paper and tuck it in the pointed top. It helps to use a real chocolate kiss as a guide.

● Small gifts can be wrapped together by dropping them in a paper towel tube. Wrap the tube to look like a piece of candy by rolling paper around the tube and tying the ends with ribbon.

● Make an elegant-looking package by wrapping a gift in white or pale colored tissue paper. Use a rubber stamp to imprint a design all over the package. Then color in parts of the design with magic markers or a gold pen. A little color will go a long way. Apply the same stamp to plain ribbon, to coordinate with the package.

Stamping with colored paint is another way to turn inexpensive tissue paper into a beautiful package. A cookie cutter makes a great design.

● If you don't have a stamp, use a black or gold pen to draw a few simple designs on the paper. Use a tiny cookie cutter as a template so that each design is the same.

● Use a pencil eraser to make polka-dot paper. Just dip it in gold paint and dot on tissue paper. You can even carve a simple design into the eraser, like a Christmas tree or star.

● Make glittered tissue paper to stuff into plain, inexpensive gift bags. Use a pencil eraser to dot glue around the edges of colored tissue paper. Sprinkle with glitter. After it dries, tuck the paper into the gift bag so that the glitter dots show. It's not necessary to cover all the paper, only the edges that will fan out of the bag.

● Fabric remnants can be cheaper than paper and a lot easier to manipulate around odd-shaped gifts. Sheer, sparkling fabrics look wonderful; or for a more masculine package, use a piece of plaid wool. Gather up the fabric around the gift. Secure with a rubber band, then tie with a ribbon.

● For really special packages, wrap the top separately so the wrapping stays in place, even after the gift is open.

● Instead of a bow, top a gift with a fresh plant arrangement. Just attach a circle of styrofoam to the top, and poke in holly or some other long-lasting greens.

● Beautiful satin and velvet ribbons purchased from the fabric store are relatively inexpensive and are a lot more elegant than the traditional craft ribbon and bows. Because they hold up so well, they can be reused over and over again.

● Use last year's Christmas cards for gift tags. Cut off the message side, and punch a hole in the upper corner of the picture. Write your new message on the back, then string a ribbon through the hole to secure.

● Instead of traditional gift wrap for small gifts, cover a sturdy little box with a piece of beautiful fabric. Pinking shears and glue are all you need. Boxes with a hinged top, such as a cigar box, work best. Some boxes can be so beautiful you won't even need a gift.

Extra large presents can be wrapped in a paper table cloth and then topped with a big outdoor bow.

● Cover a gift box with magazine pictures that reflect the gift. A box holding a new kitchen implement could be covered with magazine pictures of holiday food. Just glue the pictures on, then add a bow. Collecting the pictures is a great project for kids.

Use a spritz of hairspray to remove the price stamp from citrus fruit.

NATURAL DECORATIONS

*N*othing looks more beautiful than natural holiday decorations. Best of all, they're quick and inexpensive to make from your own backyard. Here are a few ideas.

● Small twigs can transform a dime store candle into a beautiful centerpiece. Start with a thick 8 inch candle. Gather small, straight twigs and cut them to about the same height as the candle. Arrange the sticks vertically, side by side, around the outside of the candle, and secure them with a thick rubber band or hot glue. Tie with a plaid ribbon.

● Baskets of scented pine cones make your whole house smell like Christmas. Just put pine cones in a large plastic bag and sprinkle with pine-scented oil available in craft stores. Close the bag tightly and allow them to sit for about two weeks. This makes a great gift.

● A bowl of orange pomander looks and smells like the holidays and is a great project to do with children. Pierce holes in fresh oranges in a simple design. Let children poke whole cloves into the holes. Tie the orange with a thin ribbon for more color.

● For an unusual natural decoration, use a zesting tool to carve simple designs on lemons and limes. Lightly carve swirls and curves so that the white membrane shows through the bright skin. They look and smell beautiful when displayed in a shallow bowl or basket.

● Create a tiny Christmas tree from small boxwood cuttings poked into a cone shape made from green floral foam called "oasis." (Oasis is available in craft stores.)

● Make your own pine roping using extra branches from your Christmas tree. Attach small branches to jute twine by wrapping with thin floral wire. Just be sure to overlap branches so that none of the twine shows.

String cranberries and popcorn with a needle and dental floss for a stronger garland.

● A really quick, fresh-looking wreath can be made by using a plain green artificial one as the base. Just poke in large sprigs of holly or pine and add a ready-made bow. The greens will last a long time without water, especially outdoors.

*Add a few red
bows to help
attract the birds
to your new
creation.*

BIRD TREE

fter the 25th of December, a lot of people think that Christmas trees are for the birds, and they're right. A great way to extend holiday fun and recycle your evergreen is to create a bird tree. During the long winter season, birds need food and shelter, and your old tree is the perfect solution.

● Once the ornaments are removed, take the tree outside and redecorate it for the birds.

● Kids love stringing cranberries and popcorn to create a garland of colorful food. Save dry bread to string up, too.

● Invite a few friends over to help, and you have an instant party to perk up kids during those dreary days following the holidays.

● Use dry bread slices to create ornaments. Cut them into shapes with cookie cutters and hang them from the tree.

● Use hollowed-out orange cups filled with peanut butter and bird seed. These are heavy and must be hung with wire, but the birds love them.

● Spread small dabs of peanut butter on pine cones and hang with ribbons.

● Place your tree away from the house but in clear view from a window so that you can enjoy a bird's-eye view of your wonderful recycling project.

SHOPPING THE AFTER CHRISTMAS SALES

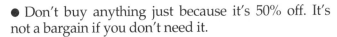

Make next year's Christmas list early and plan to shop the sales for things you really need.

Christmas can cost a bundle, but most smart consumers know how to save 50% and more on holiday shopping by planning now for next year. Here are a few reminders for taking advantage of the post-Christmas sales.

● Don't buy anything just because it's 50% off. It's not a bargain if you don't need it.

● Include any gifts you'll need in the next few months. Sales aren't limited to holiday items.

● Be sure to list teachers, coaches, co-workers, and others to whom you generally give a small token. These are the easiest kinds of gifts to find on sale.

● Elaborate ornaments are often too expensive to buy at full price, but are very reasonable at post-holiday sales.

● Make a quick check of tree lights, ornaments and other supplies. Note the things that look worn or broken. Then, not only will you save 50%, you'll save a shopping trip next year.

● Buy wrappings, bows, ribbons, and cards, but shop early for the best choices. Look for wrapping that can be used for other occasions as well.

● Look for kids' novelty pajamas and Christmas outfits. Buy a size larger and put them away for the following year.

● Even adult holiday sweaters and nightwear are often discounted.

Check out toy stores for next year's stocking stuffers.

This is the time to buy cookie cutters, holiday coffee mugs, and novelty serving pieces.

● Look for discounts on formal accessories. Evening bags, shoes, jewelry, and other things can be perfect for proms and other events later in the year.

● Look for sales on tableware and serving pieces in solid colors and designs that are not exclusively for holidays. For example, plain red or green can work all year-round.

● Infant Christmas outfits make an adorable gift anytime. Just anticipate the baby's age next Christmas.

● Shop for winter hats, gloves, scarves, and sweaters. Sizes aren't usually a problem and you can find these items marked way down.

● Watch for discounted prices on specialty items such as stationery and bath sets. These are primarily offered at holiday time, but make nice gifts for birthdays and graduations.

● Buy holiday paper products such as napkins, plates, and cups. Pick up red items for Valentine's Day and green ones for St. Patrick's day. Don't forget red, white, or blue for summer picnics.

● Novelty baking supplies and glassware are usually marked down, too.

● Be sure to make a note of what you buy in advance, and store things where you can easily find them next year.

● Start a Santa fund. Drop loose change in a holiday container all year long, and you'll be amazed at how much cash you'll have to give Santa a head start.

Entertaining

No matter how busy we get, most of us still enjoy taking the time to create a special event to entertain friends and family. When you think about it, some of our happiest memories are centered around events such as birthday parties, holidays or special family times. Whether you're planning a birthday party for a 4-year-old or a second wedding for someone past 40, here are some *Better Living* tips for a successful event.

Hand-write invitations. They're more personal and less expensive than those you buy.

ELEGANT PARTIES FOR PENNIES

*A*lthough most entertaining today is casual, certain events call for something special. Giving an elegant party can be expensive, but with a little work and creativity, it can fit into any budget. What you lack in funds you can make up in clever ideas. Here are a few.

● Set a limit. Know how much you can afford, then you can make your plans to stay within your budget.

● As a rule, stand-up cocktail parties are less expensive and easier to control than sit-down dinners, but both can be accomplished inexpensively.

● Choose a theme. A creative theme can make a party really special without spending a dime. It can be as obvious as a holiday or as simple as a color. Then plan everything around it.

● Select a date at least 3 months in advance and prepare your guest list. The more planning time you have, the more money you can save.

● Be sure to include when the party will end. This way you can better plan how much food and drink you'll need.

● Guests are part of the atmosphere. Let people know what to wear. Most parties today are casual, so people need to be reminded if you're planning a more formal affair.

● Set a time either after lunch or after dinner. Guests won't expect as much food and drink, so your menu can be light and less expensive.

● Shop for party goods on sale. After holidays, you can pick up solid-colored paper products for 50% off. For example, use black Halloween napkins for New Year's Eve or stock up on red Christmas items for Valentine's Day.

● One of the hallmarks of lavish, catered parties is elegant handmade food. You can easily do this yourself for less than half the cost. Select simple recipes and freeze ahead.

● Don't get too complicated. No party food should require more than 15 minutes of last minute preparation time.

● Create simple, elegant hors d'oeuvres by wrapping almost any filling in store-bought puff pastry.

● Alcohol is expensive, so here are a few ways to cut the cost.

Set up a water bar. Instead of alcohol, guests choose from an assortment of flavored waters. Include plain sparkling water to be mixed with fresh lemons and limes.

Try an iced coffee bar. Brew different varieties of flavored coffees and pour over frozen coffee cubes. Flavored coffee creams make drinks even more interesting.

Make your own coffee cubes in advance by freezing leftover coffee in ice cube trays.

Serve wine punch or a variety of wine coolers.

Serve only one drink, like a Mimosa, a Margarita, or a Seabreeze. This way you only have to invest in a few ingredients and provide only one kind of glass.

Don't overbuy. If you plan to toast the event with champagne, for example, count on six or seven glasses per bottle.

Inexpensive balloons and streamers are still mainstays at even the glitziest events.

● Use real china and glassware. It's less expensive and adds polish to an affair. You can usually borrow enough from friends, but if your party is large, it can actually be cheaper to rent the real thing instead of using paper products.

● Use cloth tablecloths. Paper ones are expensive and not nearly as nice as the real thing. Pretty sheets can be used as well.

● Presentation can make even the simplest hors d'oeuvres seem elegant. Invest in white paper doilies to make plain serving plates look special.

● Use your best serving pieces and borrow extras from friends.

● Create an elegant centerpiece by filling a large, clear bowl with colored ice cubes. (Make them ahead with food coloring. Experiment with shades; blue works well.) Then use the bowl to chill wine or bottles of sparkling water.

● Freeze tiny edible flowers, fresh mint, or raspberries into ice cubes. Use them for drinks or to keep foods chilled.

● Fill a tub, cooler, or sink with "frozen bubbles" to chill beer or soft drinks. In advance, fill clean balloons in bright colors with water and freeze. Don't make them too large. Then arrange in a large container to keep things cool.

● Magazine pictures that reflect the theme can be tucked into photo frames and displayed on the main table.

● Children's toys like dolls, blocks, or tiny furniture, can become a display.

● Confetti can be sprinkled on the table to add a little sparkle. Make your own by using a paper punch on old wrapping paper, foil, or bright magazine pages.

PENNY-PINCHING PARTY RECIPES

Borrow tapes or CDs from the library to provide the perfect music for the event.

EUROPEAN HERB TOASTS
Use a waffle iron to make herb toasts for hors d'oeuvres or other uses. Spread firm bread on both sides with herb butter and grill in waffle iron. Cut into bite-size pieces; serve plain or top with bits of meat or cheese.

WINE CHEESE SPREAD
In the freezer, begin saving bits of leftover hard cheese, such as cheddar. Grate in a food processor.

Add butter, wine, or beer and herb seasonings to taste.

The amounts will differ depending on how much cheese you have left over, but add a small amount at a time.

Serve as a spread with crackers, bread, or fruit.

PEACH CHEESE
Blend together cream cheese and peach preserves to taste. Tint with a bit of food coloring, if desired. Serve with crisp gingersnaps and fruit slices.

ICE CREAM MUFFINS*
1 pint leftover vanilla ice cream
2 cups biscuit mix

Blend biscuit mix and ice cream. Pour in muffin cups.

Bake at 350 degrees for about 20 minutes.

*These can also be baked in tart pans and served with ham or roast beef as cocktail sandwiches.

Allow children to help plan. Even toddlers can let you know about their favorite characters and foods.

PARTIES FOR KIDS

*K*ids' parties can be exhausting and expensive, but it's not really necessary to spend a fortune for little ones to have a good time. Here are some tips to throw a great party for pennies that's guaranteed to be fun for parents and tots.

● Invite only a few children. A common rule is your child's age plus one. So if your child is 5, invite six young guests. It's nice to invite parents, too. Not only can they help, but they'll enjoy watching their little ones have a good time.

● Let your child take part in the preparations. Making decorations, writing invitations, and other tasks can be as much fun as the party.

● Make invitations instead of buying them. It's less expensive and more fun. Hand deliver them, if it's possible.

● Plan activities. Kids enjoy parties most when the events are planned and organized.

● Line up helpers. They can take coats, help with boots, wipe up spills, help with games, and lots of other things.

● On party day, mark each child's seat with his or her name on a helium-filled balloon. Tie it to the back of the chair.

● Put a large cookie at each place setting and let kids write their names with decorator frosting to mark their place.

● Cover the party table with a white paper table cloth. Supply nontoxic markers and let kids create their own decorations. This is a great way to keep kids occupied while you're getting things prepared.

● Serve food with kids in mind. Easy-to-eat foods in fun shapes are always a hit. For example, let kids decorate individual pizza crusts with olive eyes, mushroom ears, and green pepper whiskers.

● Supply boxes of old clothes, hats, and jewelry for party dress-up.

● Take an instant snapshot of each child's outfit to send home as a party favor.

● Bake cakes in flat-bottom ice cream cones. When frosted, the cakes look just like yummy ice cream. Place cones in a muffin tin, fill about 2/3 full with batter, and bake as you would cupcakes.

● Greet guests with a yarn puzzle. Before party time, take several very long pieces of yarn, each one a different color. You'll need one piece for each guest. Take each piece of yarn and wrap it up and over and all around the house or yard. At the end of the string, tie a small gift. When each guest arrives, give them one end of the string and let them follow it until they find their gift at the end.

Then sit back and relax. Having fun comes naturally to kids. So you can be sure that your party for pennies will generate some million-dollar smiles.

Very young children are seldom good losers, so play games that allow everyone to win.

Plan way ahead. The more time you have to plan, the more time and money you can save.

KIDS' BIRTHDAY PARTIES

*E*ven people who rarely entertain are usually called on to create a birthday party or two. Today, a lot of parents choose to host a party at a restaurant or entertainment facility. But according to a professional party planner, most children claim their best birthday parties were held at home. With that in mind, here are some ideas for creating memorable celebrations without spending a lot of time or money.

● Plan the party together. Even small children will have ideas about the kind of party they would enjoy.

● When setting the time for the party, consider nap time for young children. Tired 3-year-olds are not much fun at a party.

● Have a theme and stick to it. Invitations, decorations, music, food, and games should all relate to the same idea.

● Try to incorporate as many of your child's ideas as possible. This will make the party even more special.

● Don't make a child's party too lavish. Spending too much money can destroy the charm of a child's event, and it can send the wrong message to kids.

● Develop the guest list with your child. After age 3 or 4, kids should have a lot of input.

● Expect uninvited guests. It's not unusual for a child to show up with a sibling or visiting cousin. Instead of an extra person, try to think of it as extra fun.

● Invite parents to come along with young children. They can be a big help and will love watching their children socialize.

• Smaller parties are easier to control. A good rule for the number of young guests is your child's age plus one. For example, if your child is 5, six children would be good for a party.

• Have enough adults on hand to help the party run smoothly. You'll need one adult for every four children under age 5, plus one adult for every six children older than that.

• Parties should last for approximately 2 hours. Longer parties tend to require a lot more planning and run the risk of getting boring.

• Be sure to decorate. Atmosphere is everything and kids love it. Balloons and paper streamers can really set the mood for fun.

• Make things easy. Be sure to use paper tablecloths, plates, and cups. And have plenty on hand to deal with spills, unexpected guests, and other last minute situations.

• Plan every minute of the party. Organize everything from the arrival of the first guest, to comforting the last child waiting for his mom to arrive.

• Plan to entertain early arrivals. Kids can feel awkward just waiting around. Have a helper ready to play a game while they're waiting for the activities to start. Puzzles and board games are a good idea.

• Once everyone arrives, start the party games. Sometimes activities can go very quickly, so plan more than you'll need.

• Craft projects are a great way to help kids quiet down. After a rowdy game, provide kids with a table full of supplies to create a party favor to take home.

• Try to avoid hurt feelings. Games should be designed so that everyone can be a winner.

Pace activities so that kids don't get too wound up. A hectic activity should be followed by a more relaxed one.

*Remember that
the birthday child
should get a party
favor, too.*

Entertaining

● Keep games simple. Lots of rules and confusing details take away from the fun and can really frustrate smaller children.

● Prizes should be simple, too. One idea is to give kids a sticker book when they arrive, then let them earn stickers as prizes as they play games.

● Even older kids like games. Don't expect pre-teens to entertain themselves. Organized activities take the pressure off in social situations.

● Food should be served after the games. It should be fun and plentiful. Always plan for extra guests and second helpings.

● Prepare food in advance. Kids' parties take a lot of supervision, and you don't want to be stuck in the kitchen when the kids need something.

● After the food, it's time to serve the cake.

● Instead of a single cake, it can be fun to give very young children individual cup cakes, each with a candle to blow out.

● Because most kids request "the piece of cake with the rose on top," make sure the cake has enough decorations so that each child can get one, or have extra decorations set aside to place on slices before serving.

● Instead of putting the gifts all together, have the guest of honor sit in a special chair. Then allow each child to present his or her gift, one at a time.

● Have the birthday child give a wrapped party favor to each guest so that every child has a gift to open.

● A great gift for a birthday is to offer to do a birthday book. Take pictures of the entire event and put them into a special photo album, complete with captions. This is one gift that will last a lifetime.

● If you organize an outdoor event, be sure to have a rain plan.

● Have a few basic first-aid supplies on hand for minor injuries. Novelty Band-Aids® can go along way to soothe a scraped knee.

● Plan for the unruly child. If a guest gets out of hand, take the child aside in another room and explain the rules of your home. Let the him know you're happy to have him at the party, but everyone must behave.

Plan for the unexpected. Have more of everything on hand—extra favors, food, and prizes.

Showers should be small and simple. Only the very closest friends should be invited.

BABY & BRIDAL SHOWER ETIQUETTE

*L*ifestyles have changed so much over the years that organizing a simple thing such as a bridal or baby shower can present a predicament. Although the rules have loosened up, the idea behind a shower remains the same, to honor the bride or mother-to-be, and present her with a few practical gifts to help her in her new life. But no matter how the rules may change, consideration for the guests and the guest of honor is the always best guide.

● Etiquette says that showers should be hosted by friends or relatives. It's not considered appropriate for a shower to be given by mothers or the immediate family, although they may help.

● Gifts should not be elaborate. The emphasis should be on practicality.

● As a rule, a shower is not given for second marriages. An engagement party or some other event is considered more appropriate for acknowledging the occasion.

● Baby showers are most commonly given for first children, but it is acceptable to host a shower for subsequent babies.

● If you present a gift at a baby shower, it's not necessary to give another one when the child is born.

● Although it's a nice gesture, it's not mandatory to send a gift to a shower which you cannot attend. You must, however, respond to the invitation and express your regrets.

- For financial reasons, guests should be invited to only one shower for the same event.

- Today's shower can be for women only or, when most friends are married, couples can be invited.

- Office showers can be tricky. Many people today resent feeling coerced into buying gifts for people they consider co-workers and not close friends. Keep that in mind when organizing a guest list.

- Theme showers, such as a linen shower, are a great idea when the bride or mother-to-be will be honored at more than one party.

- Post-birth showers have become an alternative to the traditional baby shower. This is a wonderful way for busy friends to visit with the new parents and see the baby all at once.

- Decorate with small gifts that can be taken home by the guest of honor. Small stuffed animals or toys can serve as a centerpiece. Pacifiers make adorable napkin rings, and baby bottles can hold pastel mints or flower arrangements on individual tables.

- At a wedding shower, kitchen gadgets are fun to use for decorating and make great party favors for guests or extra gifts for the bride-to-be.

It's considered a good idea to coordinate gifts, to be sure the guest of honor receives things that she can really use.

Start planning as early as possible. It's easier to save money if you have a lot of time.

BUDGET WEDDINGS

*S*omething old, something new, something borrowed, something blue, and a sixpence in your shoe"—which may be all the money that's left after the expense of a wedding today. Weddings have become incredibly expensive, but as anyone who's attended one can tell you, money is no guarantee of style or success. Some of the most memorable wedding celebrations have been organized for a fraction of the average cost. But no matter how much money you have, it only makes sense to be prudent about expenses. Here are some tips from experts, brides, and brides-to-be.

PLANNING

- Set a dollar limit and plan from there. It's easy to go overboard, even when you're trying to budget.

- Keep good financial records. You'll need to keep track of spending as you make arrangements, and you may need receipts if a problem develops along the way. A small notebook and shoe box will work fine.

- If you wish to be married in a particular church or synagogue, book it early.

- Look for a free location for the ceremony and reception. A private home, yours or a friend's, can be really lovely and very personal. Other possibilities include parks, botanical gardens and even historical buildings.

- Renting a tent, even a heated one, can be less costly than renting an expensive hall. And today, tents are attractive, heated and even have windows.

INVITATIONS

● Don't use oversized invitations. They can double your postage costs.

● Consider handwritten invitations that are on pretty note cards.

● Do not include a response card, guests can reply with a note of their own. The response card is a relatively new invention.

Purchase invitations from mail order companies. They tend to be much cheaper.

THEME

● Consider a candlelight wedding. Almost any location can be made beautiful with this theme.

● Borrow white Christmas lights and string them everywhere, inside and out.

● In summer, hold the wedding outside in the yard or garden filled with twinkling lights. In winter, a glowing fireplace is a beautiful centerpiece for a ceremony or reception.

● Line the aisle with luminarios—simple candles in paper bags—to make a glowing walkway for the bride and groom. If the wedding is indoors, line the sidewalk for guests.

● Place groups of votive candles on out-of-the-way tables and other safe areas.

● Have attendants or guests each hold a candle during the ceremony.

● For safety, you might consider using the small battery-operated candles. They look pretty, and are inexpensive.

● For daytime weddings, an inexpensive theme is color. A few cans of spray paint provide a cheap way to make a big impression. Paint old baskets to hold flowers. Spray-painted flower pots and vases can be used for table decorations, all in your wedding colors.

Lots of balloons and crepe paper streamers in the same color can add to the effect, all for just a few dollars.

● Color the rice. If rice is to be thrown, tint it to match the theme by mixing 1 cup water with about a teaspoon or less of food coloring. Add a cup and a half of white rice, uncooked, and allow to stand for 5 minutes. Drain and spread on a cookie sheet. Dry for 15 minutes in a 250 degree oven.

● Tie little bundles of rice in nylon net, or allow guests to scoop a handful from a beautiful serving bowl.

● Consider a holiday wedding. Your wedding will have an instant theme and you can take advantage of decorations already in place in churches and reception halls.

FOOD AND DRINK

● Hold the reception after mealtime so you won't need to serve a full meal.

● Consider a wedding tea. Usually held between 2:00 and 5:00 PM, you can serve tea sandwiches, wedding cake, tea, and coffee, with an optional champagne toast. This is usually the least expensive type of reception and can be very elegant and impressive.

● Homemade food is usually the least expensive, and very much appreciated by guests. Try to enlist the help of friends and family to prepare at least some of the food in advance.

● Here's a trick caterers use to keep costs down. Serve less expensive foods on a buffet table where guests can help themselves. Serve more expensive hors d'oeuvres from a tray carried through the crowd. This way, guests are more likely to fill up on buffet foods and only sample the special ones.

● Have catering done by students. Vo-tech programs and cooking schools will often cater events for a very reduced cost. Call early.

● Don't order a huge wedding cake with servings for everybody. It's much less expensive to have a smaller tiered bridal cake for effect, accompanied by a large sheet cake that will provide enough servings for all the guests. No one will ever notice.

Order a plain tiered cake and decorate it yourself with a few fresh flowers. (Make sure they're edible.)

● Serve only one or two beverages, such as champagne punch, wine, beer, or a single mixed drink that fits in with your theme.

● If you want to offer champagne but need to watch costs, serve guests a single glass, either as they arrive, or to toast the wedding couple.

● Toast with a Nouveau Beaujolais. This wine is drunk in the year it is made, so the vintage will be the year of your wedding. Display the bottles for decoration.

● It's not necessary to serve alcohol at all. Instead, consider an interesting water or juice bar. To make it special, use frosted or sugar-rimmed glasses, exotic fruit twists, and ice cubes with mint, fruit, and other tidbits frozen inside.

WARDROBE

● Try to purchase your wedding dress off the rack. Special orders and custom fittings can add hundreds of dollars to the cost.

● Consider a tea length or ankle length dress to avoid expensive hemming charges. An extra inch won't matter with these styles.

● To avoid extra charges, ask if your dress is available in a petite, tall, or plus version. These sizes differ in more than length, and might help to avoid complicated alterations.

● Try catalog shopping. Many catalogs offer beautiful formal dresses for a lot less than bridal salons. They're perfect for bridesmaids, and you may even find a beautiful dress in white or ivory, ideal for a bride.

Only pay for flowers. Save money by using greens from your yard and creating the arrangements yourself.

● In bridal salons, bridesmaid gowns tend to be less expensive than bridal gowns. Try to find one available in off white or ivory to use as your bridal gown.

● Rent men's formal wear from an establishment that offers a discount or free rental to the groom.

FLOWERS

● Save on flowers. Vo-tech programs often have schools of floral design that offer services at a reduced price.

● Use potted plants rather than cut flowers for decorating. These tend to be less expensive because they don't have to be arranged. They're also less delicate and can be picked up in advance.

● Use baby's breath and greens to stretch flowers. A big basket of baby's breath with a big ribbon costs a lot less than a wedding arrangement. Or fill a large container with greens and strategically tuck in a few large flowers.

● Have attendants carry a single flower or wild flowers wrapped in slender satin ribbon.

SPECIAL MEMENTOS

● Buy a few bottles of wine from the year of your wedding. Then you can save them for special anniversaries. Be sure to ask an expert about which wines will age best.

● Send an invitation to the President of the United States in care of the White House. You'll receive a lovely response, signed by the President and First Lady, which will become a family keepsake.

● If you are Catholic, send an invitation to the Pope. Ask your parish priest to help. In return, you'll receive a beautiful Papal blessing to acknowledge your wedding.

● Make a potpourri from the petals of your wedding flowers.

CATERING SECRETS

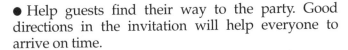rofessional caterers have lots of experience with every kind of party. They know that a successful event involves a lot more than cooking and serving food. Most admit that they've learned by making mistakes and developing solutions to prevent repeating them. Here are some of their tips to help you avoid party disasters.

In the daytime, tie balloons or a big ribbon outside to make sure guests can easily find the party.

● Help guests find their way to the party. Good directions in the invitation will help everyone to arrive on time.

● In the evening, install a colored bulb on your front porch to help guests locate the right house. Neighborhoods can be confusing at night.

● If many guests will be parking on the street, it's a good idea to alert neighbors and police to let them know when the event will begin and end.

● If the weather is bad, have someone greet guests with umbrellas for the walk from the car to the house.

● In the bathrooms, be sure to have plenty of extra supplies in full view. Parties tend to tax plumbing to the maximum, so it's considerate to place a plunger in a discrete but visible place in case of an emergency.

● Music should be a subtle addition to a party; it should not overpower conversation. Many professionals insist that it should only be played early in the evening to help get the party going, and then turned off later. Once the party begins to die down, music should be turned on again to help ease the transition.

Have a workable plan for coats and purses. Be sure guests know where to retrieve them when they're ready to leave.

● Plan to serve foods that can be made and frozen in advance. Try not to serve anything that takes more than 15 minutes of last-minute preparation time.

Plan foods that hold up well. When a party heats up, certain foods will melt or begin looking soggy.

● Plan food and drink according to the guest list. For example, young men tend to prefer heartier fare than will appeal to a group of older ladies.

● If children will be present, be sure at least some of the foods are suited to their tastes.

● Give drinks as much attention as the food. Always provide the appropriate glass for each drink, and don't forget garnishes such as lemon twists and fresh celery swizzle sticks.

● Keep beverages simple. It's not necessary to serve everything. Select beverages as you do food—choose what best fits your theme.

● When serving soft drinks or cocktails, plan for about 3/4 to 1 pound of ice per person.

● Keep ice completely wrapped while storing. Unwrapped ice will quickly take on other flavors and odors from the freezer.

● When serving champagne, plan on one bottle for each six or seven glasses.

● One standard bottle of wine will yield about six 4 ounce glasses.

● Coffee that is to be served after dinner should always be brewed a little stronger. This includes decaf.

Line natural baskets with plastic wrap to serve raw fruits and vegetables.

● Place a vanilla bean in the sugar bowl to lightly flavor the sugar for coffee or tea.

● To prevent glasses from sliding around while being carried through the party, cover the tray with a damp cloth or a piece of plastic wrap.

● Spills are common at parties, so avoid setting up serving tables near furniture that can be stained or damaged.

Red wine is never considered a cocktail, and should only be served as a dinner beverage.

● If the party will be held in a room with a very light rug, you can avoid permanent spots and stains by serving white wine instead of red.

● Don't just place food on the buffet. Use stacks of books under the tablecloth to create different levels for food presentation. Drape fabric and greens to create a soft, attractive look. Professional caters call this a "tablescape."

● Fresh flowers are a must. Instead of a prepared arrangement, buy cut flowers and arrange them yourself, reserving a few to garnish food and to accent the table. Using the same flowers will help coordinate the look of the entire buffet.

● Try to use unusual serving pieces. This will often attract as much response as the food.

● Never use a paper doily under greasy or moist canapes because they'll leave spots as they're removed from the tray. Instead, serve these foods on natural greens or a plain tray.

● Keep extra carrot and celery sticks crisp and cold by storing them in a container of ice water placed in the refrigerator.

● Keep parsley sprigs on hand to freshen trays. Store the sprigs like flowers, with stems in a jar of water placed in the refrigerator.

● A mirror makes a beautiful serving platter on a buffet table. Use it only for dry foods, to avoid any streaking or spotting.

● Always have a back-up tray for each food. The idea is to have one tray on the table and a full one in the refrigerator. When the first tray is nearly empty, whisk it away and replace it with an attractive fresh one.

Lightly spritz arrangements of raw fruits and vegetables with water to give them a fresh, dewy appearance.

● Have someone assigned to refill dips, sauces, and other dishes that will not be replaced. As containers become empty they tend to look messy on the table.

● Foods that require spreading or dipping are only appropriate for smaller groups. They're too messy and tend to hold up serving lines at large gatherings.

● For a 2-hour party, plan on about eight different types of hors d'oeuvres and allow three per person. You may need fewer if the hors d'oeuvres are substantial, and a little more if the food is very light.

● People also tend to indulge in more expensive treats like shrimp and crab, so it's important to plan for a little extra.

● When using hollowed-out fruits and vegetables as serving cups, level the bottoms by trimming a bit with a knife. Then rub their exteriors with a bit of vegetable oil and buff to give it a shine.

● For a fancier look, trim vegetables like melons and cucumbers to look like a small basket by leaving a handle across the top.

● A melon baller works well to hollow out vegetables.

● Keep dips chilled by using two bowls. Partially fill the larger bowl with water. Place the small bowl inside the large one, making sure the water comes up around the sides of the small bowl. Freeze. Remove from freezer and fill with dip. The ice should keep the dip chilled all evening.

● Blanching in lightly sugared or salted water will enhance the flavor and color of many raw vegetables. Then chill and serve plain or with a dip. Store in cold water lightly flavored with sugar or salt.

People tend to eat more when there is a greater variety of food.

● Only place one type of food on each tray. It helps to make serving more efficient, because people tend to linger while trying to make a decision.

- To make an attractive presentation, but to avoid having guests struggle with slicing large foods, place the entire food on a tray and surround it with individual portions. A wheel of cheese, for example, can be displayed while guests neatly help themselves to small, pre-cut pieces.

Candles are almost essential at a party. Add extra sparkle by placing a small mirror beneath or behind an arrangement of small candles.

- Instead of preparing individual canapes, try baking your recipe on a cookie sheet and cutting it into individual pieces.

- Use a little food coloring to tint cream cheese before you spread it on canapes.

- Save leftover fresh herbs to garnish dishes.

- Use refrigerator crescent rolls to create easy hors d'oeuvres. Wrap them around bits of meat, mushrooms, or cheese, and bake.

- Use toothpicks only when necessary, and be sure to provide an obvious receptacle for used ones. One hazard of catered parties is that guests frequently confuse discarded toothpicks for fresh ones.

- Have plenty of extra napkins placed around the party area.

- When using china plates on a buffet, be sure they're of medium weight. Thick plates, such as stonewear, are heavy for guests to hold and are unwieldy when stacking and removing from the table. Also, heavy plates tend to scratch and chip one another when stacked.

- To keep things looking neat during the party, have a few large plastic tubs tucked away in a cupboard to stow dirty trays, silver, and so on. After everyone leaves, you can pull them out and begin clean-up.

- Be sure to have plenty of garbage bags and food storage bags on hand for clean-up.

Travel

As the world gets smaller, the desire to see it seems to get bigger. Traveling to fun and exotic locations is no longer reserved for the rich. Most of us, if we put our minds to it, can manage to find clever ways to save so that we can see at least some of the world—even if we have kids! These next tips offer some ideas about finding steals, deals, and bargains in the travel industry as well as a few suggestions for getting the most out of your travel opportunities.

COURIER TRAVEL

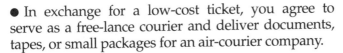here's a secret in the travel business that can save you hundreds of dollars on exotic trips. It can help you fly for half fare or less to faraway places such as Brussels, London and Hong Kong. It's completely legal, and all it takes is a little flexibility. It's called "courier travel."

The best deals are on the most exotic locations. Everybody wants to go to London, so you can expect less savings.

● In exchange for a low-cost ticket, you agree to serve as a free-lance courier and deliver documents, tapes, or small packages for an air-courier company.

● Because unaccompanied packages take longer to get through customs, couriers can save a company a lot of time.

● You'll be limited to carry-on luggage because your free baggage allowance is used for the company's cargo.

● You'll need to depart and return on specific dates, usually within 1 or 2 weeks. Here's how it works.

● You must first have a passport. If you don't have one, pick up an application at the post office.

● Courier companies provide taped phone messages that list the trips they have available, including specific destinations with departure and return dates.

● Remember, departure dates can be as little as a week away or more. The more flexible you can be, the better your chances for a cheap trip.

● You make the arrangements with a courier service over the phone, including the dates of your departure and return.

Try to be available during the off-season. There are a lot more people looking for travel opportunities in the summer.

● You then pay the company for your ticket in advance. They'll explain the procedure.

● The day of departure, you meet a company representative at the airport to receive the documents or baggage check.

● On arrival, you meet another representative and turn over the claim checks. Then you're off to enjoy your vacation.

● Most trips are from major cities. You would be responsible for your travel to the point of departure.

● Be sure to ask about cancellations and delays. Because this is not an uncommon travel problem, it's best to have a plan.

● Courier travel can save you anywhere from a few dollars to hundreds of dollars on your airline ticket. The best deals go to the most flexible. If you can leave at the drop of a hat, you have a much better chance for a great trip.

● Generally, courier companies have a need for only single travelers. It's great if you plan to travel alone, but if you'll need to make traditional arrangements for a companion, particularly at the last minute, it can be expensive.

● Call the courier numbers regularly. The trips available change regularly.

● One of the best-known companies is called "NOW VOYAGER." For a small registration fee, it will help you set up your trip. Call Now Voyager at 212 431-1616.

CRUISIN' CHEAP

*L*uxury cruises are a lot more affordable than you may think. With a little planning, you can save hundreds of dollars on your dream vacation. If a cruise is in your future, here's what the experts advise.

There are a lot of opportunities for saving in the cruise industry, so be persistent. Let your travel agent know that you're looking for value.

● Plan ahead. Most cruise lines will offer an early booking discount, which can be significant. This means booking several months in advance. If the company has not advertised a discount, be sure to ask; you may get one anyway.

● If you can't plan ahead, work with a travel agent who specializes in cruises. Have them notify you when there are last-minute specials. If you can be flexible, you can get great deals.

● Remember, a cruise vacation includes everything for one price. This includes round-trip air, transfers, accommodations, food, and entertainment.

● Travel in the spring or fall when rates are lower, or save even more during a brief economy season in September and October.

● Economy season is actually the time of year when the weather is less likely to cooperate with your vacation plans, so take this into account.

● Travel on an older ship. Regular cruise customers are always looking for new glitz and glamour, so older ships offer a better price in order to attract passengers.

Organize a group of about 15, and most cruise lines will let you travel for free.

● Decide what's more important to you, the destination or the actual cruise time. If it's the destination that interests you most, be sure to book a cruise that features maximum time in port, and don't worry so much about ship amenities.

● Plan a family reunion aboard certain ships, and the whole group can get a discount in the neighborhood of 10%.

● Ask about 2-for-1 promotions. Some cruises will have a limited number of 2-for-1 deals available.

● Book the least expensive cabin on the ship and ask about complementary upgrades. Most ships will move you to more luxurious accommodations if they're available at cruise time.

● Most cruise packages include air fare to your port of departure. Drive or use frequent flyer miles and ask for the appropriate discount.

● Cruise standby. Even luxury liners can offer substantial discounts for standby, which, in the cruise business, is about 4 to 6 weeks.

DISNEY, FAMILY STYLE

*W*ishing on a star isn't the only way to get a family dream trip to the world's most popular vacation destination. Taking the kids to Walt Disney World might seem impossible on a budget, but there are lots of ways to "minnie-mize" the cost.

Plan to arrive in the evening and stay off site that night in a budget hotel. The next morning you can move to nicer (and more expensive) accommodations, and still be fresh and ready to enjoy the park.

● Travel in the off season. Spring and Fall are ideal, because crowds are smaller and accommodations cost a lot less.

● Driving is often the least expensive way to travel, and a great percentage of Disney visitors drive there.

● Ask travel agents about special packages. Often, family tours are less expensive than organizing everything yourself. Many include air fare.

● Consider staying off-site. There are many nice hotels nearby, some with kitchens, that are quite reasonable.

● Remember that staying off-site can be less expensive—but not always. Be sure to compare prices with family-priced Disney properties.

● Staying off-site requires commuting each day in traffic and parking in a huge lot. This will take away from time spent in the park, so be sure to factor this into your decision.

● Staying on-site may not be the cheapest way to go, but there really is a lot of value.

● Disney has introduced moderate-priced resorts for families on a budget. These resorts are beautiful and provide all the convenience of a Disney hotel, without the high price. They're still not cheap, but they're well worth considering.

Have a plan. There's so much to see at Disney, it's easy to get distracted and miss the things you dreamed about. List the attractions you'd like to see each day, and make sure you do it.

● Camping is still the cheapest way to travel. Disney offers a marvelous campground with the same Disney excitement as the more expensive hotels. Call and ask about services.

● Select the right tickets. There are several to choose from so you need to compare. Make sure you only pay for the things you want to see. If you're only interested in the Magic Kingdom, for example, it's best to buy tickets for that park only. Call and ask for help in making your decision.

● Be sure to buy tickets when you make your reservations, to avoid any price increases.

● Even if you plan to stay off-site, get your tickets in advance. This way you can avoid any lines and go directly into the park.

● Get the most value for your ticket by being prepared. A lot of time and ticket value is wasted when you stand around trying to decide what to do.

● Get to the park early. Be there when the gates open and head straight for the biggest attractions. These tend to be the most popular and have the longest lines later in the day.

● Before you start, check on times for special events. Parades, fireworks, and special shows are fabulous and add to the real value of your ticket. Make sure you plan your day to include scheduled attractions. Stake out a place early enough to get a good viewing spot, and use it as a time to enjoy a snack and rest.

● Plan a re-run day. Your last day in the park should be reserved to revisit the things everyone liked best.

● Plan a picture day. Instead of lugging the camera every day, take it only on re-run day. Then you can get a photo of everyone at their favorite attractions.

- Plan a souvenir day. Save shopping until the last day and give kids a limit. You probably won't get out of the park without buying something, but this will help keep down impulse purchases.

- Eat main meals off-site when possible, but make the most of in-park meals. Disney's specialty restaurants can be as much fun as the rides and attractions. Check out your favorites and build them into your plan. Many families find that these special meal times are among the best memories of their trip.

- Make reservations in advance for a character breakfast. These are held in various restaurants. While your family enjoys breakfast, favorite Disney characters visit tables and give a little personal time to each child. It's a real highlight and a great opportunity for pictures.

- In the park, carry a water bottle or juice packs. Kids are always thirsty, and it's expensive, as well as a hassle, to keep looking for refreshments.

- Join the Magic Kingdom Club. For less than $50, you'll be eligible for substantial discounts from 10% to 30% on Disney hotels, green fees, merchandise, and even air fare.

- Buy a guidebook before you go. There are several excellent guides that go into great detail about the park and will help you better plan your trip. And don't forget to take the book with you when you go.

- But most of all, start saving now. Kids are only little once, and this really could be the trip of a lifetime. And even on a budget, a personal visit with the world's most famous mouse is worth a million.

Walt Disney World Information 407 934-7639

NOTE: *WVEC-TV is not connected with the Walt Disney Company.*

Make or buy an autograph book at home. Nearly every child who goes to a Disney park becomes excited about getting character autographs. Bring your own book and save.

Take your own stroller. Even the toughest tots wear out quickly in Florida heat, and rentals can add up.

Use a sturdy, inexpensive suitcase. Good luggage is a target for thieves.

PACKING

*W*hether it's an overnight business trip or two weeks in Europe, it seems as though the hardest part of any trip is packing. Here are some tips to help you get your stuff together.

● Try to pack in a single suitcase and carry it on the plane. You won't have to wait around the baggage claim or worry about lost luggage.

● Take only what you'll use. Here's how to do it. Plan what you think you absolutely need to take, lay it out on the bed, then only take half of that. Believe it or not, most people can do it.

● Pack shoes and other heavy items in the bottom hinged area of your suitcase so they won't slip around.

● Cushion hair dryers and other breakables by wrapping in a piece of wrinkle-free clothing.

● Soft clothing like sweatshirts should be rolled up.

● Make sure all buttons, zippers, and snaps are closed on jackets, dresses, and so on, then gently fold along natural drape of the garment.

● Tuck rolled clothing in the folds of larger things, like trousers, to help prevent serious creases.

● Use an old haberdasher's trick to pack suit jackets. Holding the shoulders, fold the two front panels, outside in, toward the back, so that they meet in the middle. The lining will show. Then fold the whole thing over once, bottom to top. It won't wrinkle.

● Pack all toiletries in separate zip-lock bags and place them in a padded kit. Air travel often causes containers to leak.

- Pack an extra plastic bag to use as a laundry bag.

- Put your name and address inside your suitcase, but for safety reasons use your business address.

- Then zip the whole thing up, and you're on your way—wrinkle free.

Tuck socks, jewelry, and small items into shoes. Slip them in narrow plastic newspaper bags for protection.

TRAVEL SAFETY TIPS

*S*ometimes a vacation can make us feel so carefree that we forget that danger doesn't disappear just because we're on holiday. Because it's always a good idea to be cautious, here are a few tips to play it safe when you travel.

● Have someone drop you off at the airport. Leaving your car in long-term parking can alert thieves that you're out of town.

● Use your business address on luggage tags. Again, don't advertise an empty home.

● Don't pack valuables such as jewelry and cameras. Keep these with you in a carry-on bag.

● Don't carry a purse. Waist packs and belt purses are a safer alternative.

● Don't walk around in a strange area after dark. Even charming tourist spots have crime.

● Use a money belt. Keep a small amount of cash in your wallet and the rest hidden in the belt.

● Be alert for pickpockets in crowds. Tourist spots are notorious for this.

● Ask for a hotel room on the second floor. In case of an emergency it will make escape easier.

● Always take your key with you. In an emergency, stairways may be blocked and you'll need to get back into your room.

● Most vacation travel is probably no more dangerous than a Boy Scout camping trip, but it can't hurt to take the Boy Scout's advice and be prepared!

When leaving a hotel room for the evening, leave the TV on and put the "Do Not Disturb" sign on the door. This will give the impression that someone is in the room and will discourage hotel burglars.

Count the number of doors between you and the nearest exit. It's common for lights to go out in an emergency. This way you can find your way to the stairwell.

TRAVEL COUPONS

*A*fter a long winter, the first signs of spring aren't always birds and blossoms. For some of us, it begins with daydreams of summer vacations. Even if you're on a budget, you can still make those travel dreams come true. One way to cut costs is by using travel-oriented coupon books. Here are a few ideas.

If you're planning a car trip, consider buying a Travel America book, which offers hotel discounts across the U.S.

● Check out entertainment travel books. These cousins to local entertainment coupon books can offer deep discounts for wonderful vacations. They often include coupons for air fare discounts that can often be applied to your best existing fare.

● Check local entertainment coupon books for special trip offers. A recent edition offered travel packages to Walt Disney World, Hawaii and Cancun—all at discount prices.

● Buy an entertainment coupon book for your city of destination.

● If you plan to visit Denver, for example, buy the Denver coupon book, and with careful planning, you can save 50% on hotels, meals, lift tickets, and other tourist attractions.

● Always make reservations through the front desk. 1-800 reservation services are usually not familiar with the best discounts available. Call the hotel directly and ask about any coupons, weekend specials, or other discounts that might apply. You're much more likely to get your best price from the hotel.

● And if you're simply interested in a quiet weekend in a quaint inn, you can buy a book offering significant savings on bed and breakfasts.

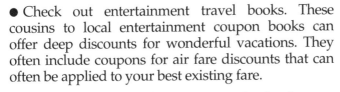

Travel Europe books offer 50% discounts for more exotic destinations.

● And to save the most, travel during the "shoulder season," which is either just before or just after a resort's busiest time. With the right timing, you can enjoy great weather while enjoying great discounts.

● Use these coupon books to "upgrade" your vacation. Instead of limiting yourself to basic accommodations, using coupons will allow you to enjoy a little luxury at budget prices.

● They say that getting there is half the fun, but for savvy travelers, getting there at half price is the most fun of all.

Around the House

*I*t's true that housework can be drudgery, but a lot of us get satisfaction from keeping things running smoothly. There's a real reward that comes from knowing how to turn a house into a home, and on a budget, no less. Most of us don't have the luxury of housekeepers or professionals to take care of the details, so these *Better Living* tips are designed to help you create a little comfort and luxury by working smarter instead of harder.

Keeping track of the age of your appliances will allow you to factor in the life expectancy the next time you have to decide whether to replace it or repair it.

APPLIANCE LIFE

*E*verybody knows that fixing a household appliance is usually less expensive than buying a new one. But fixing an appliance past its life expectancy is generally a waste of money. Knowing how long each one can be expected to perform will help you to decide when to have it repaired or when to replace it.

● Based on information from the U.S. Department of Agriculture, here are a few examples of how long you can expect an appliance to last with only basic repairs.

● A clothes dryer will last about 14 years, but you can only expect to get about 13 years from your washer.

● Gas and electric ranges should both operate for about 17 years.

● Microwave ovens can last up to 22 years, although the average is about 16.

● A basic sewing machine will keep you in stitches for about 24 years.

● A refrigerator can be expected to keep things cool for approximately 17 years.

● A dishwasher has an average life of about 10 years.

● And today's color TVs can be expected to deliver about 8 years of service.

● Remember, these are just averages and every appliance is different. Some can live long past their life expectancy. But it's always a good idea to keep track of the age of all appliances.

● Use a three-ring binder to keep all of your appliance manuals together. On each booklet, jot down the date and store where the purchase was made so you can refer to it when you have a problem.

AVERAGE LIFE EXPECTANCY OF SMALL APPLIANCES	
Coffee Maker	6 Years
Hair Dryer	4 years
Curling Iron	4 years
Toaster Oven	8 years
Answering Machine	5 years

R E F R I G E R A T O R S

A new refrigerator can cost in the neighborhood of $1,000. Add to that the cost of operation, and you're looking at a sizable chunk out of your budget. Here are a few things to keep in mind when you look at the new models.

● When deciding between repairing your old refrigerator and buying a new one, remember that a new one can pay for itself in energy savings. In a recent test, older models used double and even triple the amount of energy to operate.

● Ice-makers are convenient but displace about a cubic foot of freezer space. If you decide you need to have one, remember that a good ice maker should work fast, producing up to about 6 pounds of ice per day.

● Because of new energy-saving designs, most new refrigerators will be noisier than older models.

Once you've made your selection, here's how to keep things running efficiently.

● Try to place your refrigerator away from heat sources like stoves and even sunlight. Extra heat will cause it to work harder to stay cool.

● Keep it clean. The coils in the back gather dust, which can impede efficiency. One test revealed a 6% improvement in energy consumption just by routinely vacuuming the coils.

● Keep the gaskets clean. They often need to be replaced because of excessive mildew, and that can be expensive.

● Check to be sure your door gasket is tight. Try closing a dollar bill in the door. If it's held in tightly, the gasket is probably in good shape.

● If your refrigerator door has a magnetic seal, you should check it at night with the kitchen light off. Just place a flashlight inside the fridge, turn out the lights and look around the door for any light showing through.

Clean the door gasket regularly with soap and water, but never use bleach. Bleach can cause it to become brittle and eventually crack.

● Don't store things on top of your refrigerator. Items on top can actually block the air circulation that allows the compressor to work efficiently.

Since the typical refrigerator lasts about 17 years, these tips should go a long way toward helping you keep cool.

MICROWAVE OVENS

*A*mericans love their microwaves. About 90% of homes have one and the latest kitchen trend is to have two. Still, cooks have questions about how to choose and use a microwave oven. Here are a few tips from the experts.

● Choose a microwave with the highest wattage you can afford. The higher the wattage, the faster it will cook.

● Never cook without the glass plate inside the oven. This plate is a part of the design for proper cooking.

● Always use round cooking dishes for best results. The round shape allows the microwaves to cook more evenly.

● Never cook on a dish that is chipped or cracked. Microwaves can get trapped in the crack and cause the dish to break.

● Make sure your oven and cooking dishes are clean. Food and grease buildup can actually make your oven operate less efficiently.

● Make sure all wraps are labeled microwave safe. Many experts believe Saran Wrap® to be the most stable and safe for microwave cooking, and other brands to be much less desirable.

● Keep all plastic wraps from touching food while it is cooking.

● Slightly undercook most food. Microwaves will continue to cook for a few minutes after the food has been removed from the oven.

● Defrost properly. Too high a setting will cook the edges and leave the middle frozen. The rule of thumb is 5 minutes per pound at 30% power.

● You can expect your microwave to last 10 to 15 years. But because of changing technology, when something goes wrong, it's generally better in the long run to replace the whole thing.

● Don't worry about a microwave leaking. It's very rare unless the machine has been dropped. If you think you need a safety check, call an authorized dealer.

One microwave favorite that requires lots of power is popcorn. The higher the wattage, the better the popcorn.

HOMEMADE CLEANING SUPPLIES

*C*heck your grocery bill and you might be surprised at how much money goes to pay for household cleaning supplies. It's simply not necessary to buy specific products for each chore. A few basic cleaners, created from things you may already have on hand, can do a first-rate cleaning job while causing less environmental damage than commercial products. As an added bonus, they also save you money. Here are a few suggestions.

● Clean carpets with a mix of 1 cup cornstarch, 2 tablespoons ground cloves, and 2 cups baking soda. Leave on overnight, then vacuum.

● You can clean windows with the same basic formula as the blue cleaner. In a spray bottle, mix 2 ounces ammonia and 1 quart water.

● Many professionals recommend this method for cleaning windows. To a pail of water add a very tiny drop of Joy® liquid cleaner, just enough to break the water tension. Rub windows lightly with a very wet sponge, then go over them a wet squeegee. Keep the rubber blade of the squeegee wet and clean by wiping it each time with a damp cloth. No need to dry windows.

● Prevent steam and frost on windows by mixing 2 ounces of ammonia, 4 ounces rubbing alcohol, 1/2 teaspoon dishwashing detergent, and 1 quart of water.

● Clean copper pans with salt and lemon juice. A simple method is to sprinkle a little salt on a cut lemon and rub.

Use a typewriter eraser to clean grout in ceramic tile. Use white shoe polish to brighten grout that has discolored.

Use newspapers instead of paper towels if you like to dry windows after cleaning.

- Use baking soda to scour pots, pans, sinks, and stove tops.

- A light coating of mineral oil or baby oil will help prevent soap and water spots on stainless steel sinks.

- Disinfect toilet bowls with common household bleach. Just pour a little in and swish with a brush.

- You can also use white vinegar to clean toilet bowls. Allow it to sit for an hour or more, then flush.

- To clean chrome faucets, wipe with white vinegar and shine with soft cloth.

- Chrome that has become dull with age can be shined by rubbing with aluminum foil.

- To remove soap residue from fabric and clothing, add 1/2 cup white vinegar to the last rinse cycle. It will also remove static cling. (It's safe for most fabrics but it's always a good idea to check first.)

- Furniture can be cleaned and polished at the same time by using a solution of 3 tablespoons of lemon juice and 3 tablespoons of olive oil in 1 quart of warm water.

- Repair furniture scratches by rubbing with a crayon or shoe polish of the same color. Then polish the area with pure mayonnaise, which will allow the color to blend.

- Remove stubborn marks such as water rings from furniture by rubbing with a little toothpaste. It's just abrasive enough to work off a lot of marks without scratching the wood.

- Rub olive oil over paper that has become stuck to wood furniture. This will loosen the paper without damaging the finish.

- Remove price stickers by saturating with vegetable oil or baby oil before peeling off.

Remove rust by mixing 1 tablespoon of salt with a 1/2 of grapefruit juice. Scrub the rust with the solution, then allow it to sit. Scrub again and rinse.

Glassware can be rinsed in a solution of water and vinegar to eliminate spots and streaks.

Baking soda in the bath will help sooth sunburn and heat rash. This is especially good for infants and children.

BAKING SODA

There are some products that are so versatile that it pays to always have them on hand. Baking soda is right at the top of the list. We all know it can prevent odors in the refrigerator and, of course, it's a necessary baking ingredient, but that's only the beginning. Baking soda can replace dozens of products around the house. Not only is it effective, but it's very kind to the environment.

● Make a paste to remove coffee and tea stains from cups and counters.

● Use it to clean swimming pools. It's especially useful for kiddie pools where it's best to avoid harsh chemicals.

● Instead of spending money for specialized baking soda toothpaste, use the real thing. Just sprinkle a bit on your toothbrush.

● Baking soda can also neutralize mouth odors. Dissolve 1 teaspoon in 1/2 glass of water and swish.

● Use it to ease the pain and itching of poison ivy or bug bites. Mix it into a paste, then dab the affected area. Let it dry, then wash off.

● Cool and soothe your sweaty feet by soaking them in a solution of baking soda and water. Attack ground-in dirt, calluses and rough heels with baking soda paste and a brush.

● Baking soda can extinguish grease fires on the stove. As a safety measure, it's a good idea to keep a specially marked box of baking soda near the stove.

● Set a dish of baking soda in the microwave to absorb odors.

● Use it to freshen your carpet, especially where pets like to lie. Mix it with a few cloves, sprinkle it on, allow it to sit overnight, then vacuum.

● Remove odors from clothing by adding baking soda to your laundry. Use about 1/2 cup in the rinse cycle.

● Add a layer of baking soda under your cat litter, and it will last longer.

● Layer the bottom of your car ash tray with baking soda to keep down some of the cigarette odor.

● Use it to help remove grime when washing your car. Sprinkle it on a damp sponge, then rub the tough spots. Rinse and polish.

● Use baking soda paste to clean away corrosion build-up on battery terminals. You won't need a wire brush—with the slightly alkaline paste, corrosion is actually neutralized. Then, after reconnecting the clamps to the terminals, prevent future corrosion by wiping the terminals with petroleum jelly. Remember to use caution when working around a battery; it contains a strong acid.

Instead of scouring powders, use baking soda to clean stainless steel, porcelain, and enamel sinks.

Sprigs of basil tucked in among the fruit will help keep fruit flies away.

NATURAL BUG REMEDIES

*I*n the summer, back to nature usually means back to bugs. Because sometimes pesticides can be worse than the pests themselves, here are a few natural formulas for ridding yourself of creepy crawlers.

● Cockroach powder can be made from 1 tablespoon of powdered boric acid, about 1 teaspoon of sugar and 1 teaspoon of non-dairy coffee creamer. Mix these together and sprinkle behind cabinets and other places where roaches hide. It's relatively safe, but as with anything of this type, it should always be kept away from children and pets.

● Prevent bugs from hatching in dry goods, like flour and other grains, by freezing unopened packages for 24 hours. These tiny eggs are a natural part of harvesting and manage to stay intact throughout processing. Freezing kills any eggs that might be in the bag.

● Discourage ants from invading your kitchen by washing down any area where they might enter with full strength white vinegar.

● If you can see where the ants are coming in from outside, douse the nest with a kettle of boiling water. Another remedy is to pour ammonia on top and around the entire area.

● Ants already inside can be sprayed with a solution of water and a teaspoon or so of dishwashing liquid.

● Outdoors, treat the legs of tables with an ant repellent to keep them from climbing up and getting on the food. You can also set table legs in small containers filled with water. Ants will tumble in and drown.

- Ants can be also collected on a nontoxic ant trap. Just mix sugar, baking yeast, and molasses and spread on a 3x5 index card. Place the cards where ants travel, syrup side up. Ants will be attracted to the card and stick to it. Discard and replace when needed.

- Another ant remedy is to mix equal parts red pepper and sugar. Sprinkle it where ants travel.

- An infestation of any bugs in the house can be cleaned up quickly. Just suck them into the vacuum cleaner, then suck up some powdered bug killer. Let everything sit for awhile, then remove the vacuum cleaner bag and dispose of the whole mess.

- Fruit flies are found in decaying fruit, so keeping the fruit bowl in the refrigerator is a simple solution.

- Placing bay leaves on pantry and cupboard shelves can help keep them bug-free. A bay leaf in your flour can help prevent weevils.

- To catch a wasp in your house, just spritz him with a water mister. The water will weigh his wings down and make him easier to catch and remove.

- Crickets enter through cracks and crevices in doors, windows, and other areas of the house. If you can determine where they enter, place a strip of double-face sticky tape to catch them as they come in. Be sure to check it regularly.

- Fly paper is a simple and inexpensive way to catch flies without any effort. Just hang it in an out-of-the-way place.

- Basil, bay leaves, and mint tend to keep the fly population down to a minimum.

- To determine where mice travel, and, therefore, where to place the traps, sprinkle talcum powder or flour around possible areas of entry. Then follow the tracks.

Large sprigs of rosemary are good for moth control. They have a better chance of working if the closet doors are kept closed.

Vanilla extract, used like a perfume on your wrists and behind your ears and knees, will keep gnats away.

● A common mouse trap is still an effective way to deal with mice. Bait the trap with peanut butter.

● Incidently, if the tracks are less than 1 inch long, you've got mice. If they're about 3 inches, you've got rats.

● An old-fashioned remedy to prevent Japanese beetles from destroying roses is to liberally sprinkle bushes with self-rising flour.

● You can buy bags of lady bugs, natural enemies of aphids, to release on your rose bushes. Check your garden center.

● Citronella-scented geraniums can be purchased from a nursery. Citronella repels flies, mosquitoes, gnats, and other flying insects. Plant several near your patio to help keep bugs away.

● Plants and herbs can do a better job of repelling insects if you lightly rub the leaves to release the scent and natural repellents.

● Control slugs by placing a shallow pan of stale beer at the infested area, or just sprinkle the slugs themselves with common table salt.

● To discourage slugs from slithering under a door, pour a line of salt across the outside of the doorway. Since slugs are mostly water, the salt will dehydrate them immediately.

● A mixture of soap and water on garden plants can help control certain insects. But spray only with soap—not detergent, which can be harmful.

● A mixture of garlic juice and alcohol sprayed on plants can also be effective.

● Another recipe to curb garden pests calls for boiling six onions, a gallon of water and an entire bulb of garlic for about an hour. Cool and spray on plants.

CARPET CARE

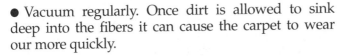

*ot long ago, carpet cleaning meant wall-to-wall work. But modern technology has made the cost of professional cleaning affordable to most budgets. Taking care of your carpet between cleanings is the real secret to keeping it beautiful. Here's what the experts say.

Don't rub. Rubbing a stain makes it larger and grinds it more deeply into the carpet.

● Vacuum regularly. Once dirt is allowed to sink deep into the fibers it can cause the carpet to wear our more quickly.

● Vacuum high-traffic areas more often—at least twice a week. This keeps the dirt on the surface and prevents it from falling deep into the fibers, where it can cause real damage.

● Avoid certain over-the-counter cleaners, especially the foamy ones. They tend to leave a soap residue in your carpet which can actually attract more dirt than you started with. A drier, granule-type cleaner is safer.

● Clean up spills immediately. The longer they sit, the better the chance of a permanent stain.

● Quickly blot up any spilled liquid. Use only a white cloth, because colors can bleed and make the stain worse.

● Spritz the spot with a little cold water to help dilute it, then blot again. Repeat this process until the stain is gone.

● Keep stains wet. If you can't remove a stain yourself, keep it moist by misting with cold water until it can be professionally cleaned. A dry stain is harder to get out.

Serving white wine rather than red at an adult party is something to help consider to prevent stains.

● Don't underestimate the value of water. Misting the spot with plain water and blotting with a clean cloth will dilute the stain and often, with patience, clean it completely.

● Don't try to clean stains with various cleaners. A number of soaps and household cleaners can chemically alter a stain and make it permanent. Frequently, professionals will discover a stain that could have been removed if the homeowner had not tried to get it out with the wrong cleaner.

● Pet stains should be blotted up with a clean towel, diluted by spraying with a mixture of white vinegar and water, then covered with another towel and heavy object to absorb the moisture.

● For wine and other high-pigment stains, gently blot the stain with a rag that has been soaked in cold water. Keep blotting until the color is absorbed by the cloth. Don't rub, because that will cause the stain to spread and become more deeply imbedded into the carpet. Mist the stain with cold water to help dilute it, then blot. Repeat.

● As with anything, the best treatment is prevention. Red fruit drinks and ice pops are nearly impossible to remove. Try training your kids to enjoy these treats away from your carpet.

● Have your carpet professionally cleaned about every six months, or more if it gets dirty.

● Be wary of cheap carpet-cleaning specials. Ask if there are any extras. Many companies make money by offering low-cost specials, then charging extra for things like spot removal and other basics.

● Check out the carpet-cleaning company. There are a lot of fly-by-nighters in this business.

● Be sure your professional carpet cleaner is experienced, as well as bonded or insured, before you agree to the service.

CLEVER CLEANING TIPS

*A*mericans continue to become more and more pressed for time. It's no wonder research shows that our homes are not as clean as they used to be. If this sounds familiar, here are a few tips from cleaning professionals and clever home-makers to help you bite the dust.

● Preventing a mess is the first line of defense. Think of ways to eliminate the biggest offenders.

● Apply a spray fabric guard to anything prone to stains. Spray sofas, chairs, kids' comforters, and anything else that needs protection.

● Put an attractive, covered basket in every room and use it as a temporary holding tank for odds and ends that would otherwise be cluttering up the room.

● Put low-pile floor mats in front of every door to catch outside dirt. Put one in front of the kitchen sink, too. Don't use throw rugs in these areas, because they're just one more thing to launder.

● In areas where you must use throw rugs, try to use them in dark colors. They show less dirt and won't need to be washed as often.

● Use arm covers on upholstered furniture, and toss an attractive afghan over the sofa back to prevent dust and stains from hair oils.

● Keep live plants in only one area of the house, to cut down on the mess from watering and feeding. Be sure all plants sit in a deep saucer to avoid any drips or spills.

● The next time you paint, be sure to select a type that is easily washable, especially on woodwork and doors.

Think about gravity and clean from the top down. Ceilings first, floors and baseboards last.

Windows are less likely to streak if you clean them on a cloudy day.

● Apply a layer of paste wax on window sills and other woodwork that is prone to fingerprints and smudges. It will stay cleaner and it will be easier to remove any smudges that do occur. This is really helpful near door handles.

● Put away all decorative items except those few you really love. Cleaning experts say that dusting, moving and replacing these things makes daily cleaning a real headache.

● Use a shower curtain instead of a shower door. It's a lot easier to clean, hides a dingy tub, and is a lot cheaper to replace.

● Keep a sponge on the soap dish to avoid cleaning soap build up. Just rinse it clean once a week.

● Install a good quality range hood in the kitchen. This device can remove about 200 pounds of dirt and grease from the air every year. That's 200 pounds that would otherwise settle in your house.

● Keep a mat or metal tray under the toaster to catch all those crumbs. Do the same under other small appliances that tend to be mess makers.

● Use foil oven protectors to prevent drips in the oven. Be sure to use them properly to avoid any damage.

● To catch oven drips, place a cookie sheet lined with foil under everything you put in the oven.

● Instead of spending time scrubbing burner trays, just buy an extra set. Pop the clean ones on and allow the grimy ones to soak clean. Burned-on grease can easily take 24 hours to soak off.

● A simple way to clean burner trays caked with grease is to seal them in a plastic garbage bag along with some ammonia. Let the whole thing sit outside and the fumes will clean off the grease. Then just wash in soap and water.

- Spray refrigerator shelves with vegetable spray and sticky spills will clean up easily.

- Cover plastic shelves with a layer of plastic wrap. Then, when spills happen, you can remove the plastic.

- Line crisper drawers with paper towels.

- Keep fresh vegetables in plastic bags with holes to allow air to circulate. If the vegetables go bad, you can lift them out of the fridge with a lot less mess.

- Store loose fruits and vegetables in plastic shoe boxes in the refrigerator. They're easy to get to and the box is easy to clean.

- Use comforters instead of bedspreads. Just pull up the covers and plump pillows.

- Eliminate top sheets on kids' beds. Most kids are very active sleepers and can end up in a tangle of sheets and covers. Invest in fitted sheets and a soft, washable comforter.

- Keep a hamper with a lid in every bedroom to avoid piles of clothes on the floor.

- Have another hamper for mending and dry cleaning. It will keep things out of sight until you get around to those chores.

- TV screens attract dust like a magnet. Wiping the screen with a fabric softener sheet will help cut down on static electricity and prevent the dust.

- Houses today are built tighter and are often closed up all day. Musty smells have become a problem for most homes. Don't wait for odors to develop. Keep your house smelling clean by airing out the house everyday. Try to open doors and windows and allow the fresh air to circulate.

Keep a dust cloth in a drawer in each bedroom. Then you can dust whenever you have a spare minute or two.

Use a hair dryer to blow dust from silk plants, lamp shades, and out of nooks and crannies such as bookcases or drawers.

● Keep your home smelling nice by saturating cotton balls with perfume, vanilla extract, peppermint oil or even a nice-smelling cleaning product. Place the cotton balls around the house in inconspicuous places. Don't forget closets and drawers.

● Spray the filter on your air conditioner with a scented air freshener and the scent will be distributed throughout your house.

● Eventually you'll need to clean, but don't do too much at once. Break jobs down into 10, 20 and 60 minute intervals.

● Eliminate clutter. Before you begin cleaning, put toys and other things away. Toss out anything that's broken.

● To save running all over the house, use a basket to collect things that belong in other rooms. Then, just carry the basket from room to room, putting things in their place.

● Instead of using a ladder, dust vaulted ceilings with a helium balloon draped with a slightly damp, light cloth. It sounds crazy but it will get those nasty cobwebs down.

● A hair dryer is also good for drying a damp and musty shower curtain.

● Static electricity causes dust to cling, so you have to dust more often. Prevent dust buildup by misting or wiping with a solution of 4 parts water and 1 part liquid fabric softener. This is especially helpful on window blinds.

● Instead of chemical sprays, mist your dust mop with a little vinegar and water. You'll have no dust and no pollution.

● Use fewer products in general. Professional cleaning companies use only a few products to clean just about anything.

● Toss a few dried beans into your disposable vacuum bag. The weight will keep the dust more compact and you will need to change the bag less frequently.

Be creative about cleaning supplies. A child's toy mop is the perfect size for cleaning in small places.

● Use your machines. Washers can launder anything made of fabric. Dishwashers can clean any knickknacks and glassware. And your dryer makes a great dust remover for drapes, pillows, and other soft objects.

● Add a few teaspoons of vinegar in your dishwater to boost the cleaning power of your detergent.

● Use a wooden toothpick to scrape the grime from the tiny crevices around the kitchen sink and stove top. It seems like a small thing, but it really makes the kitchen look a lot cleaner.

● Use a blackboard eraser to polish chrome and other metal in the kitchen and bathroom.

CARPET DYEING

Check the phone book to locate a professional company that specializes in carpet dyeing.

*I*f spots and stains have ruined your carpet, here's an idea that could save you money. Instead of replacing it, you might consider having it professionally dyed. Here's what you need to know.

● Carpets can be dyed right in your home without ever removing them from the floor.

● Most carpets made of wool or nylon can be dyed unless they've been treated to be stain resistant.

● When selecting the color, remember that the dye mixes with your present color. Generally speaking, you'll get better and more predictable results with a darker shade in the same color family.

● If you have very light carpet, you'll have more choices, but you'll still need to go to a darker shade.

● Carpets should first be steam cleaned to remove any soil or chemical residue.

● Because it's a chemical process, carpets that have been stained by pet urine or pesticides may not dye evenly.

Be aware that some older carpets with jute backing can shrink up to an inch. They should be inspected before dyeing.

● Color is intensified or darkened with each dye application. Most carpets need just one or two coats for good color. The whole process should take about an hour or so.

● To speed drying, excess moisture should be extracted after applying color.

● After 24 to 48 hours, the carpet is completely dry and soft to the touch.

● The cost of dyeing carpet can be significantly less than replacing it.

FAUX FINISHING

*L*ook in any home magazine and you'll see an elegant decorating technique called "faux finishing." It's an inexpensive way to transform ordinary walls into extraordinary art work. The method uses one or more layers of paint to create a two-toned, marbleized effect on walls. A professional job can be very pricey but, believe it or not, it's simple enough for even a beginner to do.

Sponges, feathers and other things make interesting designs in the paint.

Basically it's a solid coat of paint on the bottom, covered over with a spotted or mottled layer of another color. The "ragging off" technique is generally considered to be the easiest for beginners.

HERE'S WHAT YOU'LL NEED

Two people (It's easier to get professional results with a helper.)
oil-based wall paint
glazing liquid (available at paint stores)
roller pan
poster board (to protect ceiling)
paint roller
paint thinner
cotton rags
aluminum foil (to line the roller pan)
clear polyurethane (protective coat)

HERE'S HOW TO GET READY

● Choose two colors: the under color and the top color. The top color will be more dominant.

● Start with a solid painted wall. This will be your under color.

Practice first inside a closet or on a piece of dry wall. Although the technique is simple, you'll do better if you have a little experience.

● Many people just apply the top color over the existing paint.

● If you want a different under color, paint the wall.

● Oil-based paints tend to work best for beginners because they are more forgiving of stroke marks. They also dry more slowly, which allows you more working time.

● A glossy undercoat is easier to work with because the paint will slide around more easily.

● Mix one part wall paint with one part glazing liquid. Pour into roller pan.

● One quart of glazing liquid should be enough for an average room.

● Assemble clean cotton rags and paint thinner for soaking.

HERE'S HOW TO DO IT

● One person works as the painter and the other works as the dabber.

● The painter begins rolling the mixture on the wall. Roll two roller widths, overlapping by about two inches to avoid leaving a bare seam.

● Getting a seamless look is the secret of professional results. Make sure you don't leave a bare seam or a seam of solid color as you work.

● The dabber should follow closely behind, quickly dabbing off the paint with rags soaked in paint thinner. The more you dab, the more subtle the effect will be.

● The dabber should try to maintain a "wet edge", which means that you do not dab on the last two inches of paint until the roller can roll back over it. Again this will help avoid leaving a seam of color.

● Once the roller has applied more paint, dab the "wet edge" first before continuing along the rest of the wall.

If you make a mistake, simply paint over it and try again.

● Don't let more than one person dab the paint. Everybody has their own style and it will show up on the finished wall.

● Be sure to change the rag when it is full of paint, otherwise you'll be adding paint rather than removing it when you dab.

● To protect your work, apply a coat of clear polyurethane once the wall is dry.

A FEW OTHER TIPS

● Tape a piece of poster board to the ceiling to protect it from smudges.

● Line your roller pan with aluminum foil to allow for easy clean up.

● Make sure you have plenty of materials. It's almost impossible to get good results if you have to stop in the middle to search for supplies.

● It's also a good idea to experiment in advance with color choices.

● Remember that the top color is the most dominant. The more you dab, the less color and the more subtle the results.

● Most people find that once they finish their first job, they can't wait to try it again. Experiment with colors and different techniques for removing the top layer.

Use Velcro® to attach the remote to your favorite TV chair.

FINDING THINGS

*S*tatistics show that we spend 3 years of our lives looking for things. The busier we get, the more inclined we are to lose things. Try these little tricks to keep track of your stuff. And relax, because in a hectic world, the worst thing to lose is your sense of humor.

● Keys are the things we lose most often. Install a key hook near the door and hang keys up the minute you walk in. Or put them on a large, *very large*, key chain.

● Keep reading glasses in their place by attaching a strip of Velcro® to your glass case and the corresponding strip to your reading chair or nightstand.

● Try an inexpensive neck chain to keep glasses around your neck while you need them, and when you take them off, hang them on a special hook near your desk or reading chair.

● Velcro® also helps to keep pens in place. Glue one strip to a pen and the other strip to a note pad, the phone book, or even the phone.

● Lost contact lenses and other tiny objects can be retrieved by using your vacuum cleaner. Cover the wand with a piece of panty hose material. Gently vacuum the area where the object may have fallen and it will be trapped against the material.

● Organize the freezer with inexpensive plastic baskets to save searching at dinner time. Use one for vegetables, one for meats, and one for other things.

● To diminish the inconvenience of a lost wallet, take all your credit cards, driver's license and other important bits of information and lay them side-by-side on a copier. File copies of the information at home and at work. It won't help you find your wallet, but it will make replacing the cards a lot easier.

● Keep a lost and found basket in the front closet. Then, family members can stash things that they find lying around the house. It then becomes the first place to look when you misplace something.

● Kids get lost, too. Plan to keep tabs on them in crowded places like amusement parks or malls by dressing everyone in the same bright color. Tie helium filled balloons to little wrists, so you can spot toddlers instantly if they wander off.

BUDGET LANDSCAPING

Shop at church sales and school bazaars for cuttings and seedlings.

The secret to budget landscaping is in plant selection. While some plants are expensive and last a short time, many others are just as beautiful and, instead of dying off, will reproduce themselves and add even more beauty to your garden. Here are few tips to help you get started.

● Choose daffodil bulbs instead of tulips. Tulip bulbs will wither and die off in a few years, but daffodil bulbs will multiply and actually double over time.

● Liriope plants are excellent for defining flower beds. Five Liriope plants will become 25 or 30 in just two years.

● Daylilies multiply easily and need very little care.

● Depending on the variety, the iris can cost several dollars for a single plant, but in about two years you'll have at least twice as many and it will continue to multiply.

● Daisies are a wonderful bargain. In two seasons, an inexpensive 3-inch plant will grow to fill a square foot of your flower garden with beautiful blooms.

● For hedges, choose red-tipped Photinia or Ilex. Small plants are inexpensive and grow tall and full in just a few years.

● Consider planting fruit trees instead of ordinary shade trees. Many varieties of apple trees will grow in a small space without much care and provide shade, beauty, and bushels of apples for 20 to 30 years.

● Swap with neighbors. Many people would be happy to share plant divisions with you in exchange for cuttings and seedlings you may have.

● Another way to save money and time is to propagate existing plants the way lazy gardeners do it. Azaleas, forsythias, and even roses can be coaxed to root. Scratch or dig the soil near a plant, pull a lower branch down to the ground, cover with soil and hold it down firmly by placing a brick on top. The branch should root in about 4-6 weeks.

● Order new plants from a wholesale nursery catalog. These companies offer good prices but rarely invest in an expensive color catalog. With wholesalers, it's important to know the exact name of the plants you wish to order.

● Concentrate on perennials that can last the life of your garden. Don't waste your time replanting the same beds year after year with annuals.

● Don't spend money for a large group of perennials. Buy one or two and allow them to develop in a special area of your garden. Once the plants have grown and divided, you can transplant them in their permanent home.

● Buy plants on sale. Many garden centers try to get rid of their entire growing stock at the end of the season. Acquire healthy perennials and shrubs at a fraction of the cost, and pamper them until they can be properly transplanted.

● Shop end-of-season sales. High quality rakes, shovels, hoes, and other gardening tools can often be picked up for less than you would pay for inferior ones early in the season. Good tools will last a lifetime and can make gardening an even more pleasant experience.

● Learn to collect seeds from your plants and start your own seedlings. Once you have developed a mature garden, you should never have to buy plants again.

Put annual bedding plants in large pots rather than flower beds. They'll be easier to plant and can be strategically placed where your garden needs a little color.

Shop garage sales for gardening equipment and other outdoor items such as flower pots and garden decorations.

● Start seeds in egg cartons and other items you recycle. It's a waste to buy special containers.

● Consider wildflowers. Although you can't simply dig up wildflowers anywhere, there are responsible ways to acquire them for free. You can contact the National Wildflower Research Center in Austin, Texas for more information.

● Don't spend money on chemical nutrients. Make your own mulch pile and amend the soil with your own natural organic material.

● Get an inexpensive soil test from you local agricultural cooperative. This way, you'll know exactly what your soil lacks and you won't waste money on useless additives. You'll also give plants a better chance to thrive.

● Buy in bulk whenever possible. Seed, mulch, and even bulbs can be cheaper when purchased in large quantities.

● Pick up an old hose at a garage sale and poke holes along the length of it. Use it as a soaker hose to saturate flower beds.

CONTAINER GARDENING

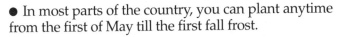he high cost of food, and a concern about pesticides, have caused a lot of people to think about growing their own vegetables. And this includes apartment dwellers. Container gardening makes it possible to grow an abundant crop of vegetables with just a few flowerpots on a sunny patio. Here's what you need to know.

Use plastic instead of clay pots because they tend to keep soil moist longer, so you'll need to water less frequently.

- In most parts of the country, you can plant anytime from the first of May till the first fall frost.

- To get started, fill a couple of large pots with commercial potting medium. It's better than soil because its lighter texture allows roots to develop more efficiently, and it is nearly always free of insects.

- You can plant almost anything in a container, but best choices for summer vegetables include tomatoes, pepper, cucumbers, squash, and eggplant.

- Place pots in a sunny location. Most vegetables need about 6 hours of sun every day.

- Water regularly, but be sure soil is dry to the touch before watering.

- Make your own mini-mulch pile. In a large garden pot, layer soil and natural material such as lawn clippings, leaves, or vegetable trimmings. As things begin to decompose, turn your mulch over once in a while with a hand spade. Once it's ready, you can add generous amounts to your plants for nourishment. Keep recycling vegetable clippings and you'll have a steady supply.

Watch out for pests. Even plants on a fifth floor balcony are susceptible to infestation. It's worth investing in some type of bug spray.

● Herbs are perfect for container gardening. You can save space by planting different varieties in the same pot. Plant varieties that you always use together, for example, oregano, chives and basil in an "Italian Mix."

● A rule of "green thumb"—if a plant's size at maturation will be approximately 30 inches high, you'll need a pot that holds about 2 gallons of soil. The smaller the mature size, the smaller the pot you can use.

● Expect a good harvest. Container gardening can yield nearly the same amount as plants in a garden. Who says you need to have a home to enjoy home grown?

HYDROPONIC GARDENING

*H*ydroponic gardening has been around since the hanging gardens of Babylon, and home systems for this soil-free technique are increasing in popularity. In fact, just about anything that grows in soil can by grown using the hydroponic method. Here's what you need to know.

You can save money by starting new plants from old ones. Cuttings are easily started in a special medium called a "horticube."

● Hydroponic gardening is basically growing plants in water instead of dirt.

● Although plants are grown in water, it's necessary to add the proper nutrients that they would normally get from the soil.

● You can buy inexpensive hydroponic kits, which include containers, nutrients, and other basics that can get you started. Once you learn a little about the technique, you can progress to a more elaborate setup.

● Plants are fed with a complete system of nutrients that you add on a regular basis. It's easier to get good results with hydroponic gardening than it is with traditional gardening in soil. That's because plants grown in dirt get some of their nutrients from the soil and the rest from fertilizer. It's difficult to gauge the proper mix.

● Hydroponic plants are generally free of soil-borne pests, so the need for most pesticides is eliminated.

● Because they grow in water, these plants develop a more efficient root system and take up less space.

● Hydroponic plants can be grown indoors or out. You can even start them outdoors in the summer and bring them indoors during the cooler months.

One of the best benefits of growing hydroponic vegetables is that the plants can take considerably less time to grow and produce.

● Vegetables grown with this method taste the same as those grown in soil.

● If your indoor light source is not strong enough, purchasing a high-intensity light system will fill in what the plant needs. Vegetable plants generally require the greatest source of light.

● Check your phone book for garden centers and shops that specialize in hydroponic gardening.

LAWN CARE

Be sure to aerate your lawn. Over time, the build up of fine mulch can become compacted.

*C*aring for your lawn can be time consuming and expensive, but certain techniques can cut down costs as well as man hours.

Instead of bagging lawn clippings, a new type of lawn mower will cut, finely mulch, and redistribute the grass as fertilizer.

The newest lawn care recommendation from the experts is to allow grass clippings to drop to the soil surface. This can save hours of work over a single season. It also means buying fewer lawn bags and putting a lot less debris in our landfills.

A new machine can be pretty expensive, but almost any lawn mower can be converted with simple adapter blades for just a few dollars.

Once you've adapted your mower, you're on your way. Here are a few things to remember.

● Mow your lawn frequently. Mulching will not work if the grass grows too tall and thick.

● Cut down on nitrogen treatments, because the mulch will naturally return nitrogen to your soil, saving you application time and money.

● Rake up any excess mulch and start a compost heap. Compost can be added to flower beds and vegetable gardens to improve the quality of the soil.

● The best time to weed your lawn is in the early spring before weeds have had a chance to flower and seed. It's also a little easier to dig out weeds after a soaking rain.

Once you've finished watering the lawn, keep the water running while you coil the hose. This way it won't kink up.

● If you water your lawn, be sure to give it a good soak. This will help it to develop a long root system that can reach deeper into the earth to get water. Light watering causes the grass to develop shallow roots which are less able to survive dry spells.

● Be careful when using any lawn chemicals. Remember that pets and children often walk on the grass with bare feet.

REGLAZING

The technique works on porcelain, fiberglass, ceramic tile, and even formica.

Remodeling a bathroom or kitchen can cost thousands, especially if you have to replace appliances or fixtures. But if the finish is your only problem, a technique called "reglazing" can save you a bundle. A grungy old bathtub can be restored to as good as new in about 2 hours for a lot less than the cost of replacing it. Here's how it works.

First, the tub is thoroughly cleaned. Then the workman etches the surface by applying an acid based solution. This prepares the old surface for the new finish.

He then applies a primer coat, which will help the new finish stick to the tub.

Then two coats of the new glaze are sprayed on the surface.

Fresh caulking finishes off the application and within 24 hours the tub is ready to be used.

● It won't last forever but the glaze has a pretty long life. Most professionals will guarantee the work for 5 years or so, but some tubs still look good 10 to 15 years later.

● The process also works well on appliances such as refrigerators and dishwashers. If a new color is all you need, it can be a lot less expensive than buying new.

Like anything, the most important thing is experience. Ask for workers' references or to see other work they've done, and then check it out.

● Colors can be custom-blended to match almost any color in the rainbow.

● To find a professional company that does reglazing check your phone book under "Porcelain Repair" and "Refinishing."

Limit the use of calling cards. Companies usually add a hefty charge per call for card use.

LONG-DISTANCE SAVING

*T*alk is cheap, but only if you're using the right long-distance company.

Choosing the best long-distance carrier can save a lot of money on long-distance calling. But most of us are completely confused by the options provided by various companies. So we don't know whether or not the savings is worth the trouble.

A consumer organization, the Telecommunications Research and Action Center (TRAC) says that the average consumer, making 15 long-distance calls a month, can save significantly by making the right choice. But because everybody's phone use is different, you need to shop for the deal that's best for you. Here are a few tips.

● Choose a calling plan, not a company. No company is always cheaper. You'll save the most money when you select a plan that best matches your own calling patterns.

● Determine your calling pattern. To do this, examine your last four phone bills. Using a highlighter, mark the time of day, day of the week, and length of all your long-distance calls. Also make note of your total monthly bill. This will give you a clear idea of how you use a long-distance service. This is also the information you'll use to compare prices.

● Then contact individual carriers and tell them your calling pattern. Ask them which of their calling plans will give you the best deal on your calling pattern. After you've checked a few companies, you can compare their prices and choose the best one for you.

● Don't just check out the big guys. Other companies, such as Allnet and Metromedia, can have great deals, too.

● Ask if the plan requires a monthly fee. Often, a plan that features low-cost calls will make up the money by adding on a monthly or minimum charge.

● Watch the clock. Most carriers drop their rates at least 35% after 5 PM and on weekends. Be sure to factor that in when you're deciding on a plan.

● Get a price comparison chart. For just a couple of dollars you can get an updated comparison chart from TRAC that lays out the cost and services of the major calling plans. To reach TRAC, write to this address:

Telecommunications Research Action Center
901 15th St., N.W., Suite 230
Washington, D.C. 20005

● The simplest tip of all is to put a timer near the phone and trim the length of your long-distance calls. Most people can save more by cutting back on the length of long-distance calls than by changing long-distance carriers.

Often florists will be happy to give you their old flowers.

POTPOURRI

*P*otpourri has become a popular way to add fragrance to your home, but even a small bag can be really expensive in a department store. Like a lot of other things, it's pretty easy to do yourself and will cost a lot less. Here's how.

● Begin by saving flower petals from your garden. Pick them after the dew has dried, but before midday, when they're less fragrant.

● Save the spent blossoms from flower arrangements, and ask friends to save theirs, too.

● Spread petals on a tray or basket, and dry them in a warm place such as an attic or closet. It should take about 2 to 7 days.

● Or, place petals between layers of silica gel (available at craft stores), which will speed up the drying process and allow flowers to retain their shape and color a little better. Just sprinkle a layer of silica gel in a cardboard box, lay flowers over the top, then cover with another layer of silica gel.

● Once you have a supply of dry flowers, you're ready to start.

● In a large bowl, mix the dried petals with spices, your choice of essential oils, and a fixative.

● A fixative simply helps the potpourri keep the fragrance longer.

● Some common fixatives are orrisroot, balsam Peru, balsam Tolu, benzoin gum, and sandalwood.

● The oils and fixatives are inexpensive and available at most craft stores.

● Oils are available in many scents, such as various florals, pine, and other natural fragrances.

● A little salt added to your mixture will help absorb any moisture and act as a preservative.

Garage sale containers are perfect for displaying and storing potpourri.

● Alcohol, such as cognac or fruit brandy, can stimulate the perfume of a potpourri, and increase its intensity.

● A few drops of vanilla extract can also be added to give a sweeter scent.

● Use a light hand with spices, so you don't overpower other fragrances.

● Let the mixture stand for a couple of weeks in an airtight container, and you'll have a perfect potpourri.

● To give your potpourri a more interesting look, you can add more than flower petals. Tiny pine cones, wood shavings, pods, and other natural things can be really attractive.

● Like any decorative touch, presentation is everything. Make sure colors, spices, and flowers coordinate with the fragrance you choose.

● Here are some simple recipes to get you started, but the real fun is when you begin to create your own.

PINK CARNATION POTPOURRI

2 cups pink carnation petals
1 cup white chrysanthemum petals
1 teaspoon cloves
1 tablespoon salt
1 ounce orrisroot or other fixative

Blend and store in a tightly covered container for about 2 weeks.

Try to blend things that will create what's called a "harmonizing fragrance."— basically, things that smell good together.

FRAGRANT PINE CONES

Fresh pine cones
a few drops pine oil

Store for 2 weeks in a large zip-lock bag.

Place the scented pine cones in a basket with a few pine branches. They look beautiful and will make your whole house smell like Christmas.

LILAC POTPOURRI

1 cup dried lilac flowers
1/2 cup wisteria blossoms
1 tablespoon salt
1/2 ounce benzoin gum or other fixative

Blend and store until well scented.

POWERWASHING

A little spring cleaning is an annual ritual for most of us. But why stop inside? Tough grime is building up outside, too. Here's an idea for cleaning your house, deck, and even your driveway. It's a simple technique that's stronger than dirt——it's powerwashing.

Powerwashing is a great way to remove mold, mildew and other dirt that can accumulate in the cracks and crevices of your home.

● Much like a car wash, powerwashing uses water that is mixed with environmentally safe cleaners, and is sprayed on your house at high pressure.

● Powerwashing is effective on brick, cedar, and sided houses, and can even be used to clean roofs that have been stained by tree sap and other debris.

● If you're planning to paint your house, a good washing can make the job easier and more effective.

● After a long winter, most wood decks are in serious need of cleaning. Powerwashing can remove the grime in just a few minutes.

● Sidewalks and driveways can also be cleaned by the same process. Paint, oil, and rust stains are the main problems. Because concrete is so porous, though, these are difficult to remove, but power-washing can make a major improvement.

● Although you can rent a machine and do it your-self, it can be tricky. Since it's relatively inexpensive to hire a professional, it's usually a good idea. Jobs are generally priced by size.

● Only use a qualified professional. Ask for, and check, references.

● Make sure they do not use bleach. It can be harmful to pets and shrubs, and can cause damage to certain types of siding.

● Make sure the company you hire is insured against any damage that might occur.

Powerwashing is a great way to make short work of the outside. Now if only someone could invent the same thing for the kitchen!

REUSE AND PRECYCLE

*N*o matter how environmentally friendly a product may be, the best way to recycle something is to reuse it yourself. Like earlier generations, we can save money and natural resources by recognizing the value of everyday things. Today we call it "precycling," which is purposely choosing things that can be reused in another way before the material is recycled. Most of us do it already, but here are a few ideas for doing more.

Use narrow plastic bags from newspapers to protect rolls of gift wrap.

PLASTIC BAGS

- Snip off a corner of a small one for use as a pastry bag.
- Use them to line trash cans and planters.
- Waterproof flashlights and radios with them for camping or weather emergency.
- Use narrow newspaper bags to fill in for plastic gloves.
- Make them into shoe protectors in your suitcase.
- Recycle them as litter bags in the car.
- You can even wash and reuse them!

ALUMINUM FOIL

- Crumple and dip in cola to remove rust from car bumpers.
- Crumple for use as a pot scrubber.
- Use as a heat reflector behind a radiator.
- Fold under a napkin in a basket of hot rolls to retain heat.

- Keep a piece with stored silver to keep silver from tarnishing.
- Wrap a piece around doorknobs when painting.
- Polish chrome on kitchen furniture, highchairs, and strollers.

BERRY BASKETS

- Use one as a small kitchen strainer.
- Use them to organize packets of mixes on a shelf.
- Nail them on a wall inside the pantry, for storing small things.
- Make them into drawer dividers to store small kitchen gadgets.
- Store lids in them for kids' sipper-cups.
- Protect a bows with them when shipping gifts.
- Use them to organize tiny doll accessories and other small toys.

CLEAN DETERGENT BOTTLES

- Use them to water plants without spilling.
- Use to add water to the Christmas tree.
- Fill them with batter to make shaped pancakes.
- Use them to dispense cooking oil.
- Make them into first-rate squirt guns.

PLASTIC SODA BOTTLES

- Make them into boot trees.
- Convert them into individual greenhouses for starting seeds in your garden.
- Cut the bottom off and use as a funnel.
- Make them into hot-water bottles.

OLD SOCKS

- Use them to store your delicate keepsakes, such as fragile Christmas ornaments.
- Store large silverware in them, such as serving spoons and cake servers.
- Make them into great dusters.
- Use them as shoe travel bags.
- Use baby socks to store jewelry in your suitcase.

BROWN PAPER BAGS

- Use them as a pressing cloth.
- Drain foods with them.
- Ripen fruit in them.
- Make them into school book covers.
- Wrap packages with them.
- Sprinkle them with salt to clean a hot iron.

Don't air-condition closets. Keep them closed when not in use.

CUTTING THE HIGH COST OF SUMMER

Your budget never goes on vacation, but when the summer arrives, so does the opportunity to spend more money. Here are a few tips to help cut the high cost of summer.

● Don't heat up the kitchen. Use energy and heat-saving appliances such as crockpots, microwaves, and pressure cookers instead of the stove. You'll stay cooler and cut energy costs by about half.

● Turn off your water heater when you go out of town, even if it's just for the weekend. In the summer, reheating the water is a lot cheaper than keeping it hot.

● Keep your freezer full. A half-empty freezer takes a lot more energy to keep cold. To fill up the space, store ice cubes, or freeze old milk cartons full of water.

● Fill extra freezer space with bags of summer fruit. You'll save about half on produce in season, as well as help keep your freezer operating efficiently. Simply lay prepared fruit on a cookie sheet, and freeze until firm. Pop it in a freezer bag and store for later use.

● Set your home thermostat at 78 degrees or higher. For each degree cooler than that, you spend an additional 6% or so in energy costs.

● Don't air-condition your fireplace opening. In summer as in the winter, fireplace openings can be a source of lost energy dollars. Close the damper and check for leaks.

● Cut back on use of toxic bug sprays. Many pests can be controlled with old-fashioned flypaper. It's cheap, effective, and best of all, safe. Just hang it discreetly out of the way and the bugs will do the rest.

T O O L   T I P S

*H*ousehold tools are a big investment, but with proper use and care they can last a lifetime. Here are a few clever tips from the experts.

Don't buy a special tool for every job. Look into renting or borrowing specialized tools.

● When purchasing a tool, a good rule of thumb is to buy a mid-priced tool. Cheap tools usually don't work very well, and the most expensive tools tend to be designed for experts. Homeowners are usually somewhere in the middle, so that's where the price of your tool should be.

● To prevent larger tools from rusting, try rubbing them with a light coat of auto paste wax. This can prevent corrosion for a long time.

● Store small tools like garden trowels in a bucket of sand. Just push the working end into the sand and leave the handle out for easy access.

● Frequently used tools should be easy to get to and kept in a closed container. Toss in a few moth balls or charcoal briquettes to help absorb moisture.

● Seldom-used tools should be sprayed with a silicone lubricant and wrapped in aluminum foil.

● Protect straight saw blades by inserting the teeth end into a slit length of old garden hose.

● To help get a nail started, just use a comb. Tuck the nail between the teeth to hold it in place, away from your thumb, until you've secured it.

● To remove a nail, get more leverage and avoid damage to your wall by slipping a magazine under the hammer.

Screws are easier to get started if they're lubricated. Push them into a bar of soap before inserting into wood.

● To start a screw in a difficult place, attach the screw to the screwdriver with masking tape. Just push it through with the sticky side up. It will hold the screw in place until you can get it started. Once the screw has penetrated the wood, you can tear the tape away.

● It also helps to tap a small hole with a nail and hammer to make an indentation before inserting a screw.

● When replacing a screw into the same hole, apply a little glue to help shore things up and keep a tight fit.

They say a poor workman always blames his tools, but with these tips that won't be a problem.

SAVING WATER

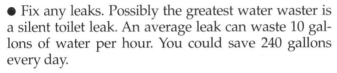

e use huge amounts of water, about 100 gallons per person per day. Experts say that most people believe they're already doing their best to conserve, but here are a few ways to get well below our extravagant average.

● Fix any leaks. Possibly the greatest water waster is a silent toilet leak. An average leak can waste 10 gallons of water per hour. You could save 240 gallons every day.

● Finding a toilet leak is simple. Put a few drops of food coloring in your toilet tank. If it shows up in the bowl, there's a leak.

● Install an aerator on your sink and reduce the flow by 50%. But the great thing is, it will seem like the flow is greater because air is mixed in with the water. An aerator is cheap and simply screws on to the end of your faucet.

● Save at least a gallon per flush by placing a weighted 1 quart bottle in your tank. Ten flushes a day could save 10 gallons. But be careful it doesn't displace so much water that you have to flush twice. You'll actually end up using more water.

● Save 10 gallons by shaving 2 minutes off your shower time. Every minute you're in the shower, 5 gallons of water goes down the drain.

● Keep a plastic bucket in the shower to catch water and use it to flush the toilet. You'll save 6 gallons every time you use it.

● Shave with a basin of water rather than a running stream, and you'll increase your water savings by 3 gallons.

● Use a glass of water to brush your teeth. Then rinse your brush in the glass when you're through. You'll save about 2 gallons.

● Save 15 gallons by running your dishwasher only when it's full. If you hand wash dishes in a dish pan rather than under running water, you'll save about the same amount.

All these tips add up to significant water savings. And at today's water prices, it's like saving liquid gold.

Good to Know

There are some things in life that are just good to know: when and how much to tip, how to tell which butter plate is yours, when to salute the flag, how to handle the hassles of car care when you don't know a lug nut from a walnut. Tips in this section are a collection of the odds and ends of life.

Attend dress rehearsals. Some groups offer drastically reduced tickets for dress rehearsals.

BUDGET ARTS

*P*eople used to believe that cultural activities were reserved for the rich. But smart consumers know you can save money on everything, even the arts. Here are some ideas.

● Offer to usher. Volunteer ushers have the opportunity to see everything, from lavish musicals to poetry readings, for free.

● Volunteer. Arts organizations always need volunteers, for everything from set construction to stuffing envelopes, and often you'll be rewarded with free tickets.

● Watch for "pay-what-you-can-night." These special performances allow you to pay just what you can afford. They're designed to encourage people to try something new in the hope that they'll come again for full price.

● Ask for group discounts. You can often save about 15% when a group of 10 or more attends the same performance.

● Check entertainment books for coupons that offer 2-for-1 discounts. Call the box office and ask where discount coupons might be available.

● Ask about senior, military and student discounts. They can be substantial.

● But most of all, go. An artistic performance enriches your life more than any bargain ever can.

KITCHEN COSMETICS

*E*ver since the days of Cleopatra, the urge to give beauty a little nudge has turned the cosmetics industry into a multi-billion-dollar business. But more than half the cost of many popular products is in the elaborate packaging and advertising, not in the product itself.

You can save a lot of money by creating your own "kitchen cosmetics." Although the glamour products like lipstick and foundation are not easily duplicated, skin and hair care products are simple to make.

KITCHEN COSMETICS GUIDE

HAIR CARE

Lemon Juice—Brings out highlights, but also conditions and shines hair.

Beer—conditions hair—apply to wet hair for more body.

Vinegar—a natural conditioner—brings out red highlights.

Warm Olive Oil— detangles and conditions hair.

Corn Meal—an effective dry shampoo, especially for oily hair. Rub in, brush out.

Flat Champagne—a luxuriant softener and hair rinse.

FACE

Cold Cream & Ground Almonds— simple skin softener and exfoliant for dry skin.

Corn Meal—finely ground, mixed with a little oil, facial lotion, or cold cream makes an effective exfoliant.

Egg White—gentle facial mask—apply to skin, allow to dry, then rinse off.

Witch Hazel—takes care of oily skin—also good for minor cuts, scrapes and shaving irritations.

Cold Tea Bags—soften the puffiness of tired eyes—sooth a painful sunburn.

Cucumber Slices—relax tired eyes and reduce puffiness around eyes.

Frozen Baby Teething Rings—soothe tired eyes.

Olive or Avocado Oil—effective makeup removers.

Plain Yogurt—creamy facial cleanser—buttermilk will work, too.

Cider Vinegar—refreshing facial splash when mixed—8 parts water and 1 part vinegar.

Baby Powder—sets lipstick and other makeup—dust on, then apply lipstick.

HANDS

Lemon & Honey—helps soothe rough skin (do not apply on broken skin).

Warm Olive Oil—soak fingers in it to soften cuticles.

Ice Water—after fingernails are painted, wait 1 to 2 minutes, then carefully soak nails in bowl filled with ice water—helps to set polish quickly and makes it more durable. (Keeping polish in the refrigerator helps to keep it fresh longer.)

BODY

Corn Meal—mixed with a little oil or lotion, soothes out rough elbows and knees.

Oat Meal Bath—soothes rough, itchy skin all over your body (pour rolled oats directly in bath water).

Olive Oil & Sea Salt—mix together and apply as a body exfoliant.

Powdered Milk—poured directly into a warm bath, conditions and soothes dry skin.

Rosemary—in a warm bath, soothes the senses and relaxes and conditions your skin.

Lemons—rubbed directly on rough spots (heels, knees, elbows, knuckles, etc.), soothes and conditions.

[This list has been approved by a physician.]

The flag should never be allowed to touch anything beneath it, such as the ground, a window sill, or shrubbery.

FLAG ETIQUETTE

*D*isplaying the American flag at home is something many people like to do on special occasions. Knowing the proper way to show the Stars and Stripes can be a little confusing. Here are a few pointers on flag etiquette.

● According to the flag code, it is the universal custom to fly the flag only from sunrise to sunset.

● If illuminated, it can be displayed at night on special occasions.

● The flag should not be flown in inclement weather and should be taken down if a storm approaches.

● The flag should be hoisted briskly, but lowered slowly in a dignified manner.

● Once removed from the halyard (that's the rope used to raise and lower it) a flag should be immediately folded and stored.

● Generally speaking, the American flag should only be flown at half-staff when authorized by the President.

● On Memorial Day, the flag should be displayed at half-staff until noon and raised to full staff from noon until sunset.

● There are about 17 official days when the flag should be flown, but, weather permitting, it's OK to fly it everyday.

● And as a patriotic gesture, many dry cleaners will clean your flag for free if you promise to fly it on Flag Day.

● Never fly a flag that is tattered or torn. A damaged flag should not be thrown away. It should be completely burned. Because this makes some people uncomfortable, the Boy Scouts and the Marines can do it for you.

OFFICIAL DAYS
TO FLY THE AMERICAN FLAG

All national and state holidays and occasions proclaimed by the President.

New Year's Day

Inauguration Day

Presidents' Day

Martin Luther King, Jr. Day

Army Day

Easter Sunday

Mother's Day

Armed Forces Day

Memorial Day

Flag Day

July 4th

Labor Day

Constitution Day

Columbus Day

Election Day

Thanksgiving

Christmas Day

A lightweight bag is less expensive. A bulky leather bag will just weigh you down.

CHEAP GOLF

Golf used to be considered a rich man's sport, but now that it's been discovered by the rest of us, here's some expert advice from a golf coach on how to save a little green on the greens.

● Order shoes and equipment from discount companies listed in the back of golf magazines.

● Don't buy new golf balls, especially if you're a beginner. You can buy used, reconditioned balls at a fraction of the cost of new ones.

● Beginners don't need a full set of clubs. To get started, you only need a few basic clubs:

number 3-5-7- and 9 irons

sand wedge

three wood

putter

● Buy clubs that are appropriate to your level of play. Beginners' games can actually be hampered by some clubs designed for higher skill levels.

● Play expensive courses during off times. Week days and later afternoons are usually cheaper. The rest of the time, play on less expensive public courses. Check the sports page for ads featuring reduced green fees.

● When possible, don't use an electric cart. Professionals know that the rhythm of walking the course can actually improve your play during a round. You'll save money and improve your game.

● Invest in lessons. An experienced teaching professional can really improve the level of your play and make the game more enjoyable. Sometimes lessons are offered through a YMCA or recreation center at a very reasonable price.

MAIL

Keep stamps on hand. If you buy them at the grocery store or by mail, you can avoid an extra trip to the post office.

The post office delivers about a half billion pieces of mail every day. It probably seems as though most of it comes to your house. If dealing with the mail has become an organizational nightmare, here are a few ideas for coping with the clutter.

● Try to handle each piece of mail only once. Decide where each piece goes and put it there.

● Toss junk mail immediately.

● Cut up any unsolicited credit cards and toss them.

● Cut down junk mail by getting off mailing lists. Just write to:

> Mail Preference Service
> Direct Marketing Association
> 11 West 42nd Street
> PO Box 3861
> New York, New York 10163-3861

● Toss magazine subscription requests or fill them out on the spot. Don't worry, you'll always get more.

● Quickly browse coupons and only save what you're sure you'll use. Throw the rest away.

● Use a basket to store catalogs. Look them over at your convenience, then toss them when you're done.

● When bills arrive, write the amount and due date on the outside of the envelopes, then put them in chronological order by due date in a special file for unpaid bills.

● Develop a simple file for all paid bills. A folding file with a pocket for each month is perfect for record keeping. File old, paid bills here.

Always use the envelopes provided in your bills. They are specially coded to speed delivery.

● Current month's bills should have two separate files, one marked PAID, one marked UNPAID. (Napkin holders work great.) This helps keep track of what still needs to be paid.

● Quarterly or yearly bills that arrive early should be filed in the UNPAID file and kept there until you pay them.

● For correspondence that requires a reply—to an insurance company, for example—copy your reply on the back of the original letter and file it away. Use either a copier or carbon paper.

● If stamps stick together, several minutes in the freezer may loosen them; if not, the post office will replace them.

● Keep a few all-occasion notes and cards on hand for birthdays and other events. Make it a part of your bill-paying chores rather than a separate errand.

Good to Know

PACKING AND MAILING

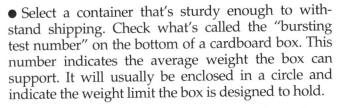

Double wrap liquids in zip-lock plastic bags to prevent any leaking.

*P*acking and mailing is a big hassle. But here are a few tips to help make things easier when you absolutely, positively have to get a package sent.

● Select a container that's sturdy enough to withstand shipping. Check what's called the "bursting test number" on the bottom of a cardboard box. This number indicates the average weight the box can support. It will usually be enclosed in a circle and indicate the weight limit the box is designed to hold.

● Cushion the contents. Use commercial products, old newspaper, chunks of styrofoam, popcorn, or crinkled plastic newspaper bags.

● Secure everything so it can't shift around during shipping. Real peanuts in the shells work great.

● Plain popcorn, packed loosely inside a cookie tin, will help keep baked goods from crumbling and help keep them fresh.

● Put a second, completed mailing label inside the package, in case the outside mailing information gets damaged.

● It's not necessary to wrap every box, but grocery bags work well if wrapping is needed. Be sure the printed side is not showing.

● Filament-reinforced tape is considered the best for securing packages.

● If you need to close a package with twine, wet it before tying. It will usually shrink as it dries and will be much tighter around the package.

Don't guess at the zip code. It's better to leave it off than to have the wrong number.

● Write very clearly. Believe it or not, each year many packages are left undelivered because the address is illegible.

● Waterproof your address. Cover it with a wide piece of waterproof tape or rub with a candle to cover it with a light coat of wax.

● Clearly indicate markings such as "fragile" and "perishable" below the postage and above the address.

● Avoid putting anything on the outside of the package other than the address and shipping directions. Cute messages or greetings can be confusing and can actually impede the delivery of your package.

TIMELY TABLE MANNERS

The fork or spoon placed horizontally above your plate is for your dessert.

*E*ven Emily Post said that "nothing is less important than which fork you use." But knowing the basics of proper table manners can make even the most casual person feel more confident at a dinner party or banquet. Etiquette is really just showing common courtesy to others, so you can usually rely on your best judgment. But here are a few things you might want to commit to memory.

● If seating arrangements have been made in advance, do not ask to be moved.

● As soon as everyone is seated at your table, place your napkin in your lap, fully open if it's a small luncheon size. A large dinner napkin should be left folded in half with the fold toward your body.

● If you must leave the table before you're completely finished, leave your napkin on the chair. A used napkin on the table signals the waiter that you won't be returning.

● Selecting the correct utensil is pretty simple. Basically you work your way from the outside in. Use the utensil on the outside first, then work toward your plate. When in doubt, watch the host or hostess to see which utensil he or she uses.

● People always get confused about the bread and butter plate. Yours is the one placed at the upper left of your place setting.

● When rolls are passed, take only one, and never butter the entire thing. Break off a bite-size piece and butter each piece as you eat it.

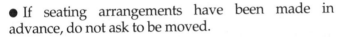

At the end of the meal, casually fold your napkin and lay it on the table.

● When eating liquids such as soup, tip the bowl of the spoon away from you. When you're finished, leave it on the saucer under your bowl.

● Stemware, such as a wine glass, is designed to keep contents cool; hold the stem while lightly supporting the bowl, to avoid warming the contents.

● Water goblets should be held with the thumb and first two fingers of your hand at the base of the bowl.

● Never refuse any food offered to you, even if it's something you don't like. Take a token portion and leave it on your plate.

● Always allow the waiter or host to pour wine into your glass. It is, however, completely acceptable to not drink it. There are two reasons for this. Your host may be planning a toast, in which case you'll need to lift your glass, and refusing wine could make others at your table feel uncomfortable for accepting it. It's subtle but nice.

● Taste your food before adding seasonings such as salt and pepper. It's considered an insult to the cook to do otherwise.

● Hold coffee cups with the index finger through the handle. No matter what you've seen in all those old English movies, never elevate your pinkie. And always keep your spoon on the saucer.

● Don't chat with the server. Pleasant greetings are fine but conversations should wait until after the meal.

● Don't assist the server unless he or she is having real difficulty.

● Elbows on the table are permissible between courses but not while eating.

● Never call attention to the mistakes of others. Being kind is the first and last rule of good etiquette.

Good to Know

T I P P I N G   S A V V Y

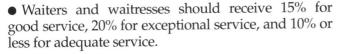

People who deliver flowers or pizza should be tipped at least $1; more if the weather is bad.

ipping can be very confusing. Although the amount should reflect the quality of service provided to you, there are some guidelines to help you make a decision. Here are suggested amounts that are generally considered appropriate when you wish to recognize good service.

● Waiters and waitresses should receive 15% for good service, 20% for exceptional service, and 10% or less for adequate service.

● Remember to tip only on the total food bill, before the tax is added.

● At a buffet, where you serve yourself, a 10% tip for the server is considered sufficient.

● Do not tip headwaiters, busboys or hostesses.

● Coat check persons should receive 50¢ to $1 per garment.

● A parking attendant should receive 50¢ to $1.

● Cab drivers should receive a 20% tip if the fare is less than $5, and 15% for a higher fare.

● Skycaps expect $1 per bag, and more if the luggage is heavy or bulky.

● At a hotel, the doorman should receive $1 if he performs a service such as hailing a cab.

● Bellboys should receive $1 per bag.

● Chambermaids deserve a $2-tip for every night you stay in your room.

● Room service should be tipped at least $1 and up to 15% of the bill.

Many grocery stores discourage tipping baggers. If it is permitted, 50¢ is sufficient.

● Some hair salons don't permit tipping, so check with the manager first. If they encourage it, tip your hair stylist 15% of the bill and $1 for the shampoo person.

SAVE THE WORLD

*F*ew of us ever get a chance to save the world, but developing some environmentally sound habits can give us a chance to preserve a bit of it. As a matter of fact, some things can actually make your life simpler. It's important that we all try to do something, because as someone once said, "This planet is also disposable."

If we all just recycled our Sunday paper, we'd save about 500,000 trees every week.

● **Clean Green.** Instead of always using chemical cleaners, start first with simple products like baking soda and white vinegar. They're effective and less expensive than commercial products. If it turns out that they can't do the job, then move up to the stronger stuff.

● **Make Mulch.** Our landfills are overflowing with lawn clippings because we foolishly throw away about 24 million tons every year. Instead of bagging them, start a mulch pile and use it to improve flower beds. You can even do it on a tiny balcony. Simply layer dirt and mulch material, like fruit and vegetable peelings, in a large planter. Turn it over every once in a while with a hand shovel. Then once it decomposes, you'll have a rich, safe fertilizer that can be used for plants and flower boxes.

● **Ban disposable batteries.** Make your new battle cry "recharge!" Rechargeable batteries can be used over and over again. All you need is a relatively inexpensive battery charger, and you can use the same few batteries for everything.

It's possible to make a big difference without making much of a sacrifice.

● **Recycle.** Even saving an occasional milk carton or aluminum can is a start.

● **Don't drive.** Cut down on unnecessary trips by calling ahead and getting information before you get in your car. Try to do business with companies located near you. For example, look for a grocery store located near a drug store, beauty shop and hardware store. Avoid special trips for errands by planning stops on your way home from work.

● **Lighten up.** Replace standard incandescent bulbs with compact florescent bulbs. They cost more, but because they last longer and use much less electricity, they're cheaper in the long run. Not only will they save energy, but one bulb will keep about a half ton of carbon dioxide out of the atmosphere.

● **Plant a tree.** Over time, a tree can remove a substantial amount of carbon dioxide from the atmosphere, and the shade can lower air conditioning costs significantly.

FITNESS ON A BUDGET

f you're like most Americans, getting in shape is at the top of your To Do List. Finding the time is one thing, but finding the money is quite another. Fitness can be expensive, so here are a few ways to trim the cost of trimming down.

Borrow or rent exercise videos before buying to make sure you like the routines. Then trade with friends to keep things interesting.

● Buy brand name athletic shoes at a significant discount from mail order companies. Look for ads in the back of various fitness magazines.

● Fancy health clubs are expensive. Consider joining the "Y" or a community center. These facilities often provide the same services for a lot less.

● Save 20% to 40% on the cost of professional quality exercise equipment like treadmills and stair steppers. A mail order company called "Better Health" works a lot like the furniture discounters. Just call with the make and model number, and they'll quote you a price over the phone—718 436-4693.

● Tape your favorite TV exercise show and play it back when the time is more convenient.

● If you're considering a diet center, watch for coupons or special deals. Always ask if it has a special rate coming up because you'll often get the discount early.

● Prepare your own diet meals. Many of the frozen diet meals feature portion control. That means you're paying more to get less. A good diet cookbook is a much better investment.

● Get free professional advice from a registered dietitian by calling the National Center for Nutrition and Dietetics at 1 800 366-1655.

Who says you can't be too rich or too thin?

Change your air filter regularly. A dirty filter lowers gas mileage.

CUTTING CAR COSTS

*A*utomobile costs could be needlessly driving up your expenses. A few simple tips from the experts may be all you need to trim the cost of getting around.

● Don't waste money on higher octane-rated gas. Use only the octane rating listed in your owner's manual. Most experts say that higher octane won't make your car run any better.

● Buy gas early in the morning. You're actually getting up to 5% more for your money if you buy gas before the heat from the afternoon sun has had a chance to warm, and thereby expand, the gas in the station's fuel tank. This is especially true in the summer.

● Don't top off your fuel tank after the automatic cut off stops the flow. In the same way gas can expand in a station's fuel tank, it can expand in your car's tank and overflow.

● Use your air conditioner. The aerodynamic design of cars over the last several years has made them extremely efficient. The drag created by lowering the windows actually requires your car to use more fuel. This is especially true on long trips at high speeds.

Drive at 55. Experts say that the average car driven at 65 mph rather than 55 mph will use 17% more fuel.

● Clean out your trunk and remove your roof rack (if it has not been factory installed). Extra weight and drag decrease your car's fuel efficiency.

● Check your tires' air pressure. You can lose 2% of fuel economy for every pound of pressure under recommended pounds per square inch. Your tires will also last longer if properly inflated.

● Don't allow an engine to idle for more than 1 minute. It takes less gas to restart.

Good to Know

CAR MAINTENANCE

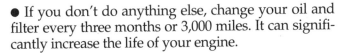

look at the cost of today's new cars is a great incentive to make your present car last longer. Experts say it's possible to actually double the life of your car by sticking to a good, regular maintenance plan. The objective is to increase your MPD—miles per dollar. Here are a few tips from the professionals.

Rotate and balance your tires about every six months or 6,000 miles. This is especially important in the winter.

- If you don't do anything else, change your oil and filter every three months or 3,000 miles. It can significantly increase the life of your engine.
- Regularly check tire pressure, but only when the tire is cool. A hot tire will read high.
- Have belts checked and adjusted periodically, and have them replaced as needed.
- As soon as possible, adjust belts that squeak when starting the car. A broken belt can lead to further damage.
- Have alignment checked and adjusted at least once a year.
- Check your cooling system every year before the summer heat sets in to be sure hose clamps are secure and the coolant is circulating efficiently.
- Every two years, be sure to check spark plugs and adjust the valves. Replace plugs about every 20,000 to 25,000 miles.
- Try to find a good, reliable mechanic whom you can stick with. Having the same technician work on your car can help to prevent a lot of expensive problems.

If windshield wipers make a lot of noise against a dry windshield, it's time to change them.

● After about 4 years or 48,000 miles, replace your timing belt. This can be a little expensive but it can mean hundreds of dollars in damage if you don't. And if it breaks while you're driving, the car will stop. A broken timing belt will leave you stranded.

These are just general requirements. Always check your owner's manual to learn what's best for your car.

Good to Know

SALVAGE YARD SAVINGS

Some salvage yards offer a computer search service. If they don't have the part, they can often locate it for you.

*P*eople are keeping cars longer today, and that means more repairs. Unless you're mechanically inclined, there's not much you can do about labor costs. But you can save plenty on parts by getting used ones from the a junk yard or salvage yard.

● As a rule, you can expect to save 50% and sometimes as much as 70% or 80% on parts from a salvage yard.

● Experts say that most used parts are as good as new. They've simply outlived the life of their original car. And they often come with a guarantee, usually about 30 days.

● You can get everything from a rear view mirror to a complete engine.

● In the old days, consumers were simply sent out to pick through a heap of old cars to find the part they needed. But in most salvage yards today, parts are conveniently displayed on shelves.

● Before your mechanic installs a new part on your car, ask if you can provide a used part. He'll let you know what to look for.

● Most salvage yards are listed in the yellow pages and will be happy to help you over the phone.

JUMP-STARTING A CAR

Jumper cables can breathe life back into your car, but only if you know the proper technique.

If you have a car, the chances are you have a battery. And if you have a battery, the chances are that one day it will die. A quick jump start can get you on your way. Here's what our experts suggest.

Position the helper car—the one that runs—so that the hood is close to the hood of the car with a dead battery.

Do not allow the cars to touch.

Turn off the ignitions in both cars.

Turn off all lights, radios and other electrical accessories.

Open the hoods of both cars. Sometimes the hood latches must be released from inside the car.

Make sure both cars have the same voltage battery. Most cars today have a 12-volt battery, but it is possible to have a 6-volt battery. A six volt battery is about half the size of a standard 12-volt type.

Locate the positive (+) and negative (-) battery terminals located on the top of the batteries.

Clip one end of either cable to the positive terminal of the helper car.

Clip the other end of the same cable to the positive terminal of the dead battery.

Then do the same with the other cable, clipping it to the negative terminals.

Start the engine of the helper car and let it run for a minute or two.

Then start the engine of the dead car.

Disconnect the cables in the reverse order that you attached them.

Allow the dead car to run for a while. It's best to drive it around for about 30 minutes or take it to have the battery recharged at a nearby service station.

CAR WASH SECRETS

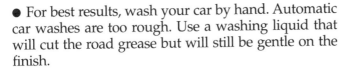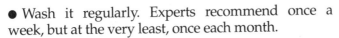ashing and cleaning your car may seem like a simple chore, but with modern finishes there's a lot more to it than just a little elbow grease. Here's what the experts say.

Don't use old rags. Use a chamois cloth instead. Old rags can be too abrasive.

● For best results, wash your car by hand. Automatic car washes are too rough. Use a washing liquid that will cut the road grease but will still be gentle on the finish.

● Wash it regularly. Experts recommend once a week, but at the very least, once each month.

● Don't use well water. Minerals are too harsh for today's finishes.

● Wash your car after it rains. Acid rain, fuel deposits, and other chemicals that come down with the rain need to be removed. If you can't wash it, at least hose it off.

● Wash one section at a time. Start in the front and work your way to the back, paying close attention to door jambs and wheel wells.

● Old towels are not recommended unless they're laundered properly. They should be washed in cold water with fabric softener.

● Wax your car every 30 to 90 days, but don't use a deep-cleaning wax because it's too abrasive.

● Inside, use a small soft brush, like a paint brush, to clean the instrument panel and all those little crevices.

● Use a dry tooth brush to sweep crumbs and debris trapped under the piping or buttons of upholstery.

● Use cotton swabs to get the dirt out of tiny places. A wooden toothpick is also a good tool for removing grime from around the gear shift and other awkward places.

● Never clean carpets with a lot of soap and water. Many of today's cars have electronics imbedded in the floor, and water can cause serious damage.

Good to Know

WINDSHIELD REPAIR

*I*nch for inch, it can be the most expensive repair to an automobile, and among the most common. The little windshield ding, caused by a flying pebble, can eventually become a large crack, and a large expense if you end up having to replace your windshield. But there's a repair technique that can save you money by fixing the nick while it's still small. The ding—or rock chip—should be repaired as soon as possible after it happens. The longer you let it go, the greater the chance it will become a crack and ruin the windshield. Here's how the repair works.

Fix a small "ding" in your windshield as soon as possible to avoid the cost of replacing the entire windshield.

Similar to a cavity in your tooth, the chip is drilled smooth and then vacuumed to remove any dust or debris.

Workmen inject a silicone adhesive into the hole, then heat the windshield to pull the mixture securely into the opening.

Once the nick is filled, it's treated with ultraviolet light to cure the adhesive and complete the repair.

The entire process takes only about an a hour.

Although the process is great for most nicks, it can distort driving vision, so it should never be used in the acute area of a driver's view.

It's also not appropriate if your windshield is electronically heated, if the chip has penetrated the windshield's lamination, or if the damage covers more than a 2-square-inch area.

So don't let a little windshield damage chip away at your budget. Because, as they say in the business, they can fix almost any ding.

Acknowledgments

Had I known this book was going to be so much work, I might not have started it. But it's certain I never would have finished without the help of many wonderful people. My grateful thanks go to the entire Community Affairs staff at WVEC Television for their ability to take on an additional project of major proportions, and continue to function without skipping a beat.

Sincere thanks to Lee Salzberger, a gifted leader with a genuine commitment to community and family issues.

Thanks to Bud Brown for his dedication to quality and his enthusiasm for innovation.

My appreciation to Wendy Juren, the producer of Better Living, *for being a person who knows a little something about nearly everything, and possesses the ability to track down information on anything else.*

Thank you to Dru Doyle, Linda Wiley, and Lauren Yee for their many contributions to the project.

David Cassidy for his support of a unique project.

David Smith for his editing expertise and unwavering support.

Special thanks to the Virginia Cooperative Extension for providing materials and advice.

Thank you to the many experts who so willingly contributed their expertise and advice in all matters covered in this book.

Special appreciation to Susan Mayo, Home Economist and Vice-President of Consumer Affairs for Farm Fresh Grocery stores, for her savvy understanding of what consumers really need to know.

Bonnie Heimbach, Extension Agent, for her great common sense and enthusiasm for this project.

Mark Maund, auto service and technology instructor, for turning the mysteries of auto care into simple tips for the mechanically challenged.

Acknowledgments

Carolann D. Brown, author and financial advisor, for stressing the importance of basic money management in building financial security.

Malcolm and Rachel Fries, Certified Financial Planners, for helping to make solid financial information accessible to the average person.

Albert Cicconi, M.D., for his genuine commitment to providing clear, basic health information to the public.

To Annette Overlease and Frances Dodson for their design expertise and good humor under pressure.

To Katherine Smith and Anna Banana for their patience and inspiration.

Thanks to Jill Vaden and Anne Thomas for their dedication to perfection in proofing and editing.

Thanks to Mary Jane Barnes, image and etiquette consultant.

And to all the people who value the importance of homemaking and have contributed many of the tips and ideas in this book.